MANAGEMENT AND LEADERSHIP IN EDUCATION SERIES

Series Editors: PETER RIBBINS AND JOHN SAYER

Rethinking Education

LEEDS BECKETT UNIVERSITY
LIBRARY
Leeds Metropolitan University

17 0171518 X

TITLES IN THE MANAGEMENT AND LEADERSHIP IN EDUCATION SERIES

Rethinking Education

The Consequences of Jurassic Management

HELEN GUNTER

CASSELL

Cassell

Wellington House
125 Strand
London WC2R 0BB

PO Box 605
Herndon
VA 20172

© Helen Gunter 1997

All rights reserved. No part of this publication may be reproduced or transmitted in any form or by any means, electronic or mechanical, including photocopying, recording or any information storage or retrieval system, without prior permission in writing from the publishers.

British Library Cataloguing-in-Publication Data
A catalogue record for this book is available from the British Library.

ISBN   0-304-33867-2 (hardback)
           0-304-33868-0 (paperback)✓

Typeset by Action Typesetting Ltd, Gloucester
Printed and bound in Great Britain by Redwood Books, Trowbridge, Wiltshire

LEEDS METROPOLITAN
UNIVERSITY LIBRARY
1701751 8X ✓
CPB
562732
371.2 GUN
14.5.97   £11.99

Contents

This book is dedicated to the memory of
Mary Elizabeth Stanton
20 December 1924 – 3 January 1985

Preface

This book is an invitation to all those working in the field of education management – as practitioners, lecturers, trainers, consultants or inspectors – to join with me and face a challenge. It may be a surprise, but the challenge is not one conceptualized as being external to education management in the form of new legislation and new policy initiatives, but a challenge that comes from the business of education management as an industry with a clearly defined market and a constantly improving product range. Education management has grown rapidly in the last ten years to the extent that it is an industry driven by the market with ever-changing products in the form of books, courses and contract work. Here is an opportunity to stand back and take a reflexive approach and ask questions such as:

- Does education management have a history?
- Does education management have a future?

I say that this is a challenge because these types of question are not being asked in the journals and books dedicated to education management. However, they are being asked elsewhere, and if education management is to be more than the market-driven product that it is being characterized as, then such questions require exploration.

This book is an invitation for a number of reasons: firstly, it is inevitably a personal view, as some of my concern is the product of being directly involved in the business of education management in different guises during the last fifteen years – as a teacher, a lecturer, a student, a manager, a researcher, a consultant and an inspector in education. Secondly, it is also a product of personal change in moving from teaching in a school into higher education. I have been the 'expert-teacher as manager' in a school, and I have been the 'expert-manager as teacher' in higher education. My move to Keele University has brought me into contact with a new perspective, especially the importance of theory, a huge range of ideas which have facilitated a different type of reading, a different type of networking and the cultural context in which reflection and reflexivity are nurtured.

At this stage you may be forgiven for thinking that this book is pure self-indulgence as I navel-gaze and produce an entirely subjective account. Yes, there are more questions than answers, because I do not – and should not – provide the answers. This is not avoiding the obvious; any answers I provided would be my answers, and it is the arrogance of the problem-solving focus of education management that is central to my questions. Therefore the third reason for the invitation is that the answers (and of course new questions) are with you: if I ask questions about the history of education management then that history lies with you, as a fellow writer, or researcher, or teacher who is doing a part-time master's degree, or Office for Standards in Education (OFSTED) inspector, or as a member of the British Educational Management and Administration Society (BEMAS).

Education management is not external to you but is deeply embedded in your portfolio of work and the approach you take to that work. In this sense the book is a metaphor for the Chaos Theory theme: the butterfly effect! Therefore I am flapping my wings and such a small input (sensitive to local conditions) could cause a 'storm' in which those involved in education management begin to ask different questions about what they are doing and more importantly why they are doing it. Such questions might be:

- Why am I, as a consultant, going to recommend the creation of self-managing teams to a college as a part of its restructuring programme?
- Why am I, as an OFSTED-registered inspector, going to make evaluation and monitoring a key issue for action in a school's report?
- Why am I, as an education management lecturer, going to use systems theory to teach marketing?
- Why am I, as an appraisal co-ordinator in a school, going to write a staff development plan?
- Why am I, as a HE employee, bidding for contract research?

If practitioners are undertaking these management tasks then perhaps we should be asking why, and what are the consequences for their lives and work? I am particularly interested in the legitimacy of the teacher as manager. The evangelical drive of the managerialist project so evident within education management products is rooted in the promotion of management language, tasks and culture, and the marginalization of pedagogy, subject and professional collegiality. Teaching becomes a technology that can be observed, deconstructed, analysed, costed, measured and packaged. While the right to manage has been decentralized to educational institutions as a part of public sector restructuring, knowledge creation has not. Management is about information for decision-making, efficiency indicators and policy statements. It is not about who wants to know these things and what for. Furthermore, management is not about what is happening in the lives and work of teachers and pupils, and how they are connected to the structural injustices integral to society and the economy. The teacher as manager is neutralized, apolitical and therefore cheated. In proactively building teams, we establish a consensus-seeking framework in which control is through membership surveillance of each other to ensure that external agendas are being met.

The ongoing manufacture of books, courses and multimedia packages gives the observer the impression that these products are an essential requirement for teachers, especially for those in, or aspiring to, leadership roles. Is this appearance of control evident in reality, or are the complexities of real life within schools too rich and diverse (so far) to resist? Have teachers bought the message along with the book or the course? Education management is very seductive, and the promise of reprofessionalism through managerial competences is very tempting within a climate where private sector practices are valued. Certainly teachers are legally required to conform to managerial strategies, whether it is in formulating an OFSTED Action Plan or administering SATs. What is fascinating is the extent to which teachers subvert, fudge and resist these developments as being contrary to the teaching and learning process. At the very simplest level, is the fact that I am marking exercise books at midnight because I'm inefficient and can't prioritize, or because I spent my non-contact time with a child in need?

I do not want to be a critic of education management for the next hundred pages or so, such that the reader is passively offended or takes negative action to counter the criticisms in all kinds of forums. Rather, the book is about exploring together some of the key questions concerning education management, and I would welcome a dialogue beyond these pages in which you flap your wings. As Wheatley (1994) has stated,

> It is natural for any system, whether it be human or chemical, to attempt to quell a disturbance when it first appears. But if the disturbance survives those first attempts at suppression and remains lodged within the system, an iterative process begins. The disturbance increases as different parts of the system get hold of it. Finally, it becomes so amplified that it cannot be ignored. This dynamic supports some current ideas that organizational change, even in large systems, can be created by a small group of committed individuals... (p.96)

We are all participants of the Education Management Industry, whether we write, read, watch, act or think about flyers, adverts, books and trainers. As a consultant, lecturer or trainer you may view yourself as approaching your role with an ethical dimension and commitment to work with teachers in facilitating learning and development. So do I. This is not in question. Our views and beliefs about this are not right or wrong, rather this book is concerned with asking questions: Where do we obtain our beliefs about education, schools and teachers? How do we act in relation to those beliefs? What choices have we made at different times in our professional lives about how we engage within the educational process? Who do we network with, and is it a reciprocal relationship? Do we always present the management model as being the only and superior model available for teachers?

The main criticisms that could be levelled at this book are that it is about yearning for a world that has gone, and therefore at best we should humour the author until she catches up, or at worst we should declare her a heretic and a misguided victim of the academic snobbery that pervades certain educational journals and institutions. This book is not about exposing a rather expensive con trick by the new right, managerialists or whoever; nor is it a product of Luddism or nostalgia. It is about stimulating a debate within and about the business of education management in which participants can and should participate. Is management an inevitable and accepted hegemony or an area of debate and controversy? A reflexive approach to my own biography has brought me to the question: what is the purpose of education management?

Helen Gunter
Keele University, February 1996

Acknowledgements

Chapters 2 and 5 build on work that has already been published (Jurassic management: chaos and management development in educational institutions, *Journal of Educational Administration*, 1995, **33** (4)), and I am grateful to MCB Press for permission to re-use it here. I would like to thank Professor A. Ross Thomas for his insight and support in the original development of the article.

Excerpts from Michael Crichton's *Jurassic Park* (copyright © 1990 by Michael Crichton) and *The Lost World* (copyright © 1995 by Michael Crichton) are reprinted by permission of Alfred A. Knopf Inc., New York.

I would like to thank Professor Denis Gleeson for giving me the encouragement to turn my ideas into a book. I am deeply indebted to Professor Jenny Ozga for her inspiration and for encouraging me to think out loud. I would also like to thank Horace Bennett and Sylvia Reid for reading an early draft of the book and providing me with stimulating feedback. Of course I take full responsibility for the views expressed.

Finally, I would like to thank my family for putting up with my long absences in front of the computer. A huge thank-you to Barry for his support and for patiently listening to all that follows in this book.

CHAPTER 1

Extinction?

Current orthodoxy in management text and training is the human resource management model, which has its origins in the excellence and quality models of US business writings. This book investigates the potential failure of what it labels 'Jurassic Management': visioning, consensus value systems, proactively created teams and development planning. The book uses a metaphor based on Michael Crichton's (1991) best-selling adventure novel *Jurassic Park*, in which the failure of the theme park can be seen to illustrate serious weaknesses in the field of education management. It would be useful for those participating in the field of education management to reflect on the following observation made by Davies (1992):

> I cannot believe that hundreds of headteachers, whose professional and job satisfaction has come through working with teachers and children so that they can walk along the road towards empowerment and liberty, can so quickly swap all this for the keyboard, spreadsheet and bank balance. Post 1988, we seem to have entered a new era of managerialism without ever being clear what it is that we are managing. It may be over simplistic to characterise the many dimensions of the headteacher's role into two giant ledgers, but if we take one substantive column to being the 'leading professional' and the other being 'the managing director', then so much of our re-orientation since the end of the last decade has led us to serving the mythical customer, who is thought to have an insatiable appetite for statistics and league tables, and providing information for the board of governors. (p.3)

So is the burgeoning of education management as publications, courses and expert consultants a symptom of, or actually responsible for, these types of changes? The growth of the management imperative is so often presented as an optimistic and positive development in schools and colleges that it almost seems strange to raise questions about it. While we may consider that there have been benefits for teachers as a result of educational changes, we do need to consider what may have been lost and how teachers can understand how professionalism is being reconstructed by the management project. In doing this, I am reminded of *The Lost World* (Crichton, 1995; the sequel to *Jurassic Park*, Crichton, 1991), in which the scientists look at a recreated prehistoric ecological system to see if there are any clues to explain why dinosaurs became extinct. What is clear from reading this in combination with Lewin (1992) is that environmental change (e.g. food, weather or an asteroid) is important but not the only cause. Crichton (1995) puts forward a theory of extinction in which

> after every major environmental change, a wave of extinctions has usually followed – but not right away. Extinctions only occur thousands, or millions of years later. Take the last glaciation in North America. The glaciers descended, the climate changed severely, but animals didn't die. Only after the glaciers receded, when you'd think things would go back to normal, did lots of species become extinct ... And when the environment goes back to normal, it's not really a return to normal. In evolutionary terms, it's another big change, and it's just too much to keep up with. I believe that new behavior in populations can emerge in unexpected ways. (p.193)

What is being argued here is that adaptation to the environment is not just physical but behavioural, and behaviour can change quickly, and can be for better or for worse. If we apply this to the field of education management then we can explore the environmental context within which it is located, and consider the complex behaviour patterns within it. Central to this is learning: how do participants within the field of education management behave? What options do they have open to them? What choices do they make? Why? What networks do they construct? What knowledge is generated and for what purpose?

The debate that I want to encourage within and about education management is one that will focus on the factors that could cause both the field and participants to become extinct. Here extinction may not mean 'death' in the sense of the closing of schools, the redundancy of trainers and the end of *Management in Education* as a practitioner forum. Rather, it is about a way of working and a way of looking at the world that is currently being destroyed by the weight of the managerialist agenda. As Crichton (1995) further argues:

> All extinction theories are based on the fossil record. But the fossil record doesn't show the sort of behaviour we're seeing here. It doesn't record the complexity of groups interacting. (p.192)

If education management was to shut up shop tomorrow what would be left to dig up, analyse and reconstruct about life within the field in the 1990s? We would be left with course leaflets, validation documents for master's programmes, evaluation forms for in-service days and do-it-yourself manuals on how to manage your school. If schools and colleges are to be judged by their outcomes then perhaps we should do the same for education management. However, this book is also about complexity and chaos as a means by which participants within the field of education management can reflect on the research and theoretical base of the management strategies that are being sold to practitioners. This raises further interesting questions: surely you don't expect practitioners to be so gullible as to accept what we read, hear and are exhorted to do? If that is the question that practitioners are currently asking themselves then it is greatly reassuring, and what is of particular interest to me is whether the endurance of professional leadership among teachers and lecturers means that we talk more about management than we actually perform it in order to fulfil the requirements of external agencies.

Furthermore, as history shows, new agendas, projects or revolutions do not wipe out behaviours, values and attitudes. Instead resistance in all its forms can enable the longevity of what can, at different times, be considered to be unacceptable norms. Therefore the complex behaviour of educational professionals is central here, and changes in the environment need not lead to changes in behaviour; the growth of managerialism need not lead to a growth of the management function within schools and colleges. The managerial revolution is not, and cannot be, a foregone conclusion. As Newman and Clarke (1994, p.26) have argued, it is a 'contested domain', and the field of education management has to ask itself what type of contribution it is making to the debate.

The Education Management Industry

Education management is defined as 'a field of study and practice concerned with the operation of educational organizations' (Bush, 1995, p.1). It is a lively and energetic field that is international in its focus and networking. It is a field in which some very important research is being done into how schools and colleges currently work, particularly by working with practitioners on issues to do with change and development. Much of this work is published in books and conference papers, and in prestigious journals in the UK (e.g. *Educational Management and Administration* and *School Organisation*) and abroad (e.g. *Journal of Educational Administration*) by colleagues (too numerous to mention) with national and international reputations for scholarship.

However, what is of concern is what I have come to label as the Education Management Industry, which is manufacturing management products that are different in tone, language and content to what was being published in the 1960s and 1970s to help educational professionals bring about change. There have been times in the last decade when I have felt alone in my worries and concerns about what I have seen unfolding, and it has been encouraging to discover that questions are being raised about what is happening to the field. Towards the end of compiling my ideas for this book I discovered Davies (1990), who states:

> Am I (a) alone, (b) paranoid or (c) forward-looking in finding the idea of management-by-ticklist a sinister and dehumanizing development? (p.17)

No you are not! Furthermore, Smyth (1993) is baffled by what the Caldwell and Spinks (1988) concept of *The Self Managing School* actually represents and the agenda on which it is based. Smyth (1993) states:

> What occurs, of course, is a cultural shift away from education to management and other forms of entrepreneurialism. We lose sight of what it is that is being managed, and what we have is the replacement of a professional model of education with what is a largely discredited industrial management model. Why we in education would want to emulate this kind of derelict model that failed so demonstrably as evidenced in the corporate excesses of the 1980s is a complete mystery. (p.7)

What is a complete mystery to me is why the Education Management Industry has colluded with this process and has made teachers feel that their professional skills are redundant and that their judgement is not to be trusted. There is a lot of current education management thinking and writing that focuses around people issues such as ownership and empowerment; systems issues such as quality; structural issues such as decentralization, and self managing teams; and, finally, task issues such as product and performance outcomes. This is in direct contrast to the 1960s when writing and thinking on what was then termed educational administration can be characterized as seeing people as professionals working in decision-making systems and structures that were focused on supporting the professional in the classroom, and in the pastoral care of children.

The Education Management Industry has grown very rapidly since 1988 and is concerned with the identification, marketing and selling of products such as books and folders, courses, videos and multimedia packages. What these products all have in common is that they are concerned with do-it-yourself guidance on how to solve management problems within educational institutions. Some are presented in the traditional book format, others are presented in a folder and are often called handbooks or manuals. It is what Halpin has called 'management by ringbinder' (1990, p.474), and Angus (1994, p.79) labels 'survival guides'. I have spent a lot of time reading these products and you will probably be familiar with many of them, e.g. Caldwell and Spinks (1988) *The Self Managing School* and (1992) *Leading the Self Managing School*; Hargreaves and Hopkins (1991) *The Empowered School: the management and practice of development planning*; plus the nine books in the *Issues in Management* series (see page 66). In addition you have only to look at the book review pages in journals to gain a sense of just how big the industry is. For example if you look at volumes 6–9 in *Management in Education* you will see that of the 250 or so publications that have been reviewed, at least half are within the umbrella of 'management by ringbinder' and to purchase the lot would set you back over £2,000. This is a lucrative and busy industry with around 25,000 copies of *The Self Managing School* and 12,000 copies of *Leading the Self Managing School* having been sold worldwide.

What characterizes the education management product is the emphasis on so-called good practice, common sense and how useful the strategies are. A useful metaphor is that of *recipes* in which the products are lists of ingredients plus a method which, if followed, will delight your staff and customers. Kent (1989) tells us:

> If you follow the advice offered it should help you to organise and run your school smoothly and efficiently. This will leave you time to make that personal contribution to the school which is the main function of all good headteachers. It should provide you with a number of short-cuts to making your school a good one in the terms by which, rightly, these matters are judged in the community's opinion. (p.10)

Some products do accept that you might want to alter the ingredients or change the order of the method, but this is left to you to experiment with and perhaps seek additional training. Alternatively, we could see the products as *maps*, in which the terrain of management problems has been discovered for you and the solutions to keep you on the right road and heading in the right direction are presented in a neat, easy-to-follow package. Whichever metaphor is used, what is central to these products is the portrayal of certainty. If the strategies are followed then problems will be avoided or solved according to your management needs. The reader or course participant is often told that the author or trainer is at the 'leading' or 'cutting' edge of new strategies for the educational institution of the next century. The beliefs of the authors tend to be explicit so that you know what type of product you are buying, and the whole tone evinces confidence and you are exhorted into trusting the systematic processes described. Books and folders contain proformas to fill in, checklists, key questions for action, do's and don'ts, simple diagrams showing clear relationships, and new competences are presented through narrative descriptions, case studies and exercises.

The business of managing a school or college is all pervading and you can purchase handbooks that are generic or sector specific (Aylett, 1991; Barker, 1991; Craig, 1989; Davies *et al.*, 1990; Davies and Ellison (eds), 1994; Green (ed.), 1993, 1994, 1995; Marland (ed.), 1986; McMahon and Bolam, 1990; and Playfoot *et al.*, 1989); or that are more specialized: appraisal (Bennett *et al.*, 1992; Bollington and Bradley, 1991; Jones, 1993; Mathias and Jones, 1989); budgets (Davies and Ellison, 1990); inspection (Ormston and Shaw, 1994); the law (Adams, 1993); marketing (Davies and Ellison, 1991; Marland and Rogers, 1991); planning (Davies and Ellison, 1992; Puffitt *et al.*, 1992); self-management (Trotter, 1993); senior management (Smith, 1992); special needs (Walters, 1994); teams (Bell, 1992); and time (Knight, 1989). Education management is doing for education what Haynes manuals have done for home car maintenance, and Dr Hessayon has done for amateur gardening. While education management products have some value, and I admit to reading the 'top tips' and guidance in 'agony columns', we do have to admit that it is hardly the way to run a national service staffed by very highly educated professionals. We need to see such products within the policy context and the effect they are having on teachers' lives and their work. Hargreaves (1994) has touched on this issue when he states:

> In England and Wales, policymakers tend to treat teachers rather like naughty children; in need of firm guidelines, strict requirements and a few short sharp evaluative shocks to keep them up to the mark. In the United States the tendency is to treat and train teachers more like recovering alcoholics: subjecting them to step-by-step programs of effective instruction or conflict management or professional growth in ways which make them overly dependent on pseudo-scientific expertise developed and imposed by others. (p.xiv)

Humour very quickly gave way to despair when reading about the importance of handshaking in marketing the school, and jumble sales in income generation. This technical and rational approach to social processes reminds me of the 'cult of efficiency' identified by Callahan (1962) in the education system in the USA in the 1930s, when trivia became central to education administration publications. Callahan (1962) reports the work of Cooke *et al.* in their book *Principles of School Administration* (1938), in which the following advice is given on dusting:

> All pupils' and teachers' desk-and-seat equipment should be dusted thoroughly every morning before the opening of the school. Flipping a feather duster or dust cloth across desks is not effective, and only moves the dust from one place to another. If vacuum equipment is not available, the only satisfactory method of dusting furniture is to wipe the surfaces thoroughly with a cloth or especially prepared sanitary duster. In dusting, the janitor should take straight strokes with the grain of the wood. (Callahan, p.243)

We need to ask if the tragedy that Callahan (1962) identified as happening in the USA in the 1930s is unfolding in England and Wales at the current time. The Education Management Industry must take responsibility for the current situation in which the teacher finds him/herself within its emphasis on how the current policy context provides new challenges for teachers which mean training in new skills and knowledge, and acquiring a different understanding of the purpose of schools. According to the Education Management Industry the policy context means a management imperative and an inevitable problem-solving approach.

Jurassic Management: seduction

The growth of the Education Management Industry is linked to the policy context. Government policy and recent legislation clearly has a management imperative for schools and the public sector in general based on business management models. The White Paper *Better Schools* (DES, 1985) focuses on two issues in education: standards and value for money. Within this the central role of industry and commerce is emphasized:

> Industry and commerce are among the school's main customers. They have a

vital role in raising standards at school by explaining their needs to the education service and by taking part in the development of its policies and activities.
The Government will continue to invite industry and commerce to participate
in national discussions of objectives, and in the work of national committees
concerned with school education. It looks to firms to involve themselves at
other levels, notably in the work of school governing bodies and examination
boards. (para 296, p.88)

The importance of industry and commerce in education in pursuit of
higher standards and value for money has grown with the development of
Training and Enterprise Councils (TECs) and vocational curriculum initiatives. Furthermore, the restructuring of education in the form of self-
managing and self-governing schools and colleges has increased the role of
industry and commerce by involvement on governing bodies through to
financial investment. This latter issue is illustrated in a booklet produced by
the Department for Education (DFE), *Education Means Business* (1994). The
booklet is designed to publicize the Government's Private Finance Initiative
(PFI) launched in 1992, and is aimed at informing the private sector about
the investment opportunities in educational institutions. As Gillian
Shephard in the Foreword states:

> The Government has introduced radical policies to raise standards achieved
> by pupils and students; and to promote efficient management of schools
> and colleges. The Private Finance Initiative can play its part in helping to
> achieve these aims. It offers opportunities to broaden the base of capital invest-
> ment in education, and to introduce skills, ideas and management practices
> from the private sector. The goal is a more effective environment for learn-
> ing. (p.1)

This is equally endorsed by Howard Davies, Director General of the CBI:

> Our aim through the Private Finance Initiative is to find ways to bring more
> private sector investment into the educational sector. For this to make commer-
> cial sense the private sector will have to contribute its management skills. For
> new investment it will also be necessary for the private and public sector to work
> together to generate new, additional revenue streams to ensure a return on the
> investment. We have seen an appetite in the private sector to invest in other
> elements of the nation's infrastructure with the full encouragement of govern-
> ment. The time has now come to see what progress can be made in education.
> (p.2)

What is interesting about these statements from the Secretary of State and
the Chair of the CBI is that they encapsulate the key policy developments
in the 1980s/1990s and set the agenda for the future:

- The emphasis on efficiency, effectiveness and economy linked to
  standards and excellence. This is illustrated in all aspects of
  government policy (e.g. OFSTED inspection, role of the Audit
  Commission and performance league tables).
- Sources of funding for education are based on the marketplace
  through attracting business investment to projects such as

building a joint-use leisure centre or a conference centre. This fits in with the market approach to the funding of schools and colleges in relation to consumer choice, be it parents or post-graduates.

- Education is conceptualized as a part of the infrastructure of the economy and this fits in with government policy on the national curriculum at Key Stages 1–3 and vocational curriculum at Key Stages 4–5 and beyond.
- The management of educational institutions is seen as needing business management skills, in which attracting and working with private sector investors will enable their development.
- The broadening of the capital base for education through private sector investment is linked to the overall policy of privatization from the 1980s. This can be seen in the context of prolonged economic decline and the crisis in the capitalist state, and ideological goals about the role of the state from the New Right.

Government agencies promote management skills and knowledge through their own 'management-by-ringbinder' products: from the Audit Commission's *Adding up the Sums* (1993), which is prescriptive about its approach to finance; through to OFSTED's (1992) *Handbook for the Inspection of Schools*, which accepts and promotes visioning and development planning.

The Thatcherite approach to the public sector has been privatization combined with the managerialist restructuring of the residue, and as Pollitt (1992) has argued it is a New Right agenda where

> private-sector disciplines can be introduced to the public services, political control can be strengthened, budgets trimmed, professional autonomy reduced, public service unions weakened and a quasi-competitive framework erected to flush out the 'natural' inefficiences of bureaucracy. (p.49)

While the Education Management Industry continues to be preoccupied with issues to do with knowledge, skills (or should I say competences) and understanding rooted in 'how do you manage?', then it is failing to see the growth of managerialism as a part of a bigger political project. As Clarke *et al.* (1994) have argued, we need to understand the link between the managerialist agenda and power:

> managerialization constitutes the means through which the structure and culture of public services are being recast. In doing so it seeks to introduce new orientations, remodels existing relations of power and affects how and where social policy choices are made. This is why the new public sector management matters. (p.4)

The Education Management Industry has accepted the changes in power relations as creating not only the urgency for a management imperative but also its superiority. Those within the Education Management Industry have found it difficult to resist as the logic of the managerialist language and skills are attractive. Newman and Clarke (1994) have shown:

> Management has been identified as a transformational force counterposed to each of the old modes of power. By contrast with the professional, the manager is driven by the search for efficiency rather than abstract 'professional standards'. Compared to the bureaucrat, the manager is flexible and outward-looking. Unlike the politician, the manager inhabits the 'real world' of 'good business practices' not the realms of doctrinaire ideology. In each of these areas, the manager is also more 'customer centred' than concerned with the maintenance and development of organizational 'empires'. (p.23)

There are myths and stories which abound concerning what it was like before the introduction of local financial management (LFM) and local management of schools (LMS). We were all critics of aspects of public bureaucracy and for many the television programme *Yes Minister* was not really a comedy but was so close to the truth that it was charting the tragedy of the British state. Reform was clearly an imperative, but did it have to be a managerial one? This question is never asked within education management products, and, in attempting to replace the professional with the manager, education management has failed to recognize key factors:

- public services are complex
- the provision of those services is instrinsically connected with the lives and work of those who provide them;
- professional claims to standards, judgement and status have been characterized as privileged in order to bring teachers (and other public sector workers) under control (Newman and Clarke, 1994, pp.28–9).

Furthermore, Newman and Clarke (1994) go on to show the 'hollowness' and 'emptiness' of managerialism:

> It is derived from management's position as a recipient of devolved social and economic power – historically rooted in the separation of ownership and control in private enterprise. In that sense, management possesses no superordinate goals or values of its own. The pursuit of efficiency may be the mission statement of management – but this is efficiency in the achievement of objectives which others define (ideally, competitiveness and profitability as prescribed by the enterprises's owners). (p.29)

Goals and values inherent within professionalism, and which have always been evident within the teacher or lecturer, or the school or college, have been ridiculed and downgraded. The practitioner and educational institution are now in receipt of the goals and values determined elsewhere from the market, or from external agencies such as the School Curriculum and Assessment Authority (SCAA), the Teacher Training Agency (TTA), OFSTED and the Further Education Funding Council (FEFC). Education management products have tried to deal with this by discovering the management of values. If we accept Everard's (1995) assertion that 'values are inescapable: we do not choose them; they claim us' (p.131), then the key issue for him in understanding organizational behaviour is how people develop 'a sense of' values and how 'the shaping' of values takes place. He is an advocate of 'values mapping', provides a checklist of eleven values processes and endorses the trend in competency statements and accreditation. While the pluralism of values is accepted, what is absent is a discussion about how management values are extrinsic and are ' viewed as functional, shared and essentially integrative' (Clarke *et al.*, 1994, p.235). Education has always been rooted in values but what is being advocated is a shift from teacher–pupil–parent discussion of belief and bonding to a validation of whether teachers have the capability to believe and to provide an evidence base so that it can be measured and proved.

Fergusson (1994) has argued that a business value system in education is flawed because the teacher's knowledge, skills and values are rooted in teaching and learning, with motivation and reward intrinsically linked to this. While teachers are involved in achievement and development the conceptualization of this as scores, grades and league tables is of little value. For teachers, extrinsic values in which education is a product that should be deconstructed, costed and measured is an anathema. Is there capacity for resistance within the profession? How long can the profession continue to raise questions about the national curriculum, testing and resources? Will senior management teams be seduced further by managerial knowledge and competences in order to exercise managerial control and accountability? Professional identity is a problem that time is rapidly overcoming in favour of the managerialist state:

> Long established conceptions of roles, duties, rights and responsibilities are deconstructed in the face of resentment, resistance, low morale and scepticism. The least amenable leave or retire, the most mouldable enter at the bottom of the profession. The process of reconstruction is only as strong and resilient as the overt reforms which drag it in their wake. As sceptical teachers submit to *force majeure* and comply with the National Curriculum programmes of study, test their pupils, accept appraisal, as reluctant heads sit on sub-committees of governing bodies to apportion the schools' budgets etc., they come gradually to live and be imbued by the logic of new roles, new tasks, new functions and, in the end, to absorb partial redefinitions of their professional selves, first inhabiting them, eventually becoming them … As redefinition takes hold, though, it is likely to be deep-seated and long-lived. The greatest sources of resistance will have departed, redefinitions will not be easily undone, and as young recruits who never knew any different move up the hierarchy the consolidation of the new regime can bed in.   (Fergusson, 1994, p.113)

Where does this leave the Education Management Industry? Perhaps it is time to stand back and reflect on how managerialism within the public sector is reshaping and reconstructing what we are doing and why we are doing it. It is out of the remit of this book to engage in an in-depth investigation into the link between government policy and the growth of the management imperative – that has been done very effectively elsewhere (e.g. Ball, 1987, 1990a; Elliott and Hall, 1994) – but what is both pertinent and interesting is that in facing legislation and new policy initiatives we could ask the question: who have teachers turned to for help? Clearly, they have turned to their own profession (e.g. local education authority (LEA) advisers, higher education lecturers and researchers, and retired heads and deputies who have become independent consultants). We might have reasonably expected co-professionals to have enabled teachers to build on existing knowledge and skills, and to retain the culture of professional judgement and standards. As the market floods with 'management-by-ring-binder' materials, through to a wealth of courses and training events from LEAs, independent consultants and higher education, then we wonder how long professional educational leadership can resist. Every week in the *Guardian* and the *Times Educational Supplement* we see courses on how to effectively implement an aspect of government policy from appraisal to inspection, and more recently a heavy emphasis on school improvement and effectiveness as a new cash cow in the market. According to Lawrence (1994), 49 universities and four colleges offer masters courses in education management and are competing within a crowded marketplace for customers. As Fergusson (1994) has shown:

> Management training designed to provide these has burgeoned in a variety of forms, from the instrumental to the still remarkably academic and reflective. There are clear signs that the tide is running strongly from the latter to the former. The most pronounced evidence of this is the growth of interest in MBAs specifically designed for teachers. Broadly, these tend to be focused more on the means than the ends of management, and are as such more evidently compatible with a managerialist approach. (p.107)

The concern about the end of 'academic and reflective' approaches to professional development is illustrated by the large number of institutions that have sought approval as Headlamp (Headteachers' Leadership and Management Programme) providers, and the trend towards competency-led training for current and aspiring headteachers. Of course an interesting question might be: to what extent has registration as a Headlamp provider affected or determined in-service and course provision? Registration could be merely the satisfaction of an internal or external requirement rather than signifying agreement or collaboration with the scheme. If so, then what is making higher education do this? Is it the case with other activities? Are books being written to serve other purposes than the target audience on the cover? Is it that all the conferences and courses advertised in the weekly education press are not recruiting and therefore do not happen, but they have to be constructed and advertised?

What has happened in the 1980s and 1990s is the growth of educational management providers to support educational institutions in how to manage in a turbulent environment. These providers are partly made up of institutional-based professionals who teach on postgraduate courses in educational management, provide consultancy and in-service for educational institutions and work for government agencies such as OFSTED and SCAA. Some providers have been seduced by the evangelical and superior tone of the management project. Others have been forced into promoting the management model by the very managerial context within which they work. Managerialism has come to higher education with a vengeance and has undermined the professional context of researchers and lecturers. Work is organized and costed through accountability matrices with internal markets. Externally the lecturer/researcher is forced to become a trainer, where the performance is as good as the last evaluation form filled in by course participants, and income generation targets are seen as measures of effectiveness. The Research Assessment Exercise (RAE) means that contract research and the measurement of outcomes in the form of publications can be more important than method. As Maguire and Ball (1994) have argued:

> In higher education, the insertion of a market ideology has also had a major impact. Institutions have been set against one another, bidding in competition for student numbers and funding, and encouraged to undercut one another in desperate attempts to survive. The situation in smaller colleges, polytechnics, and new universities has become serious. This sector is typified by low morale, reduced conditions of service, more teaching, less time for research, but pressing needs both academically and financially to attract funded research. The financial and academic agendas of higher education are increasingly at odds ... (pp.269–70)

Combined with these developments in higher education has been the growth in the number of independent consultants who have taken early retirement or been made redundant from educational institutions. They are often part-time lecturers in higher education, and work also in providing in-service and for government agencies. Consultancy in secondary schools is a growth area (Glover and Law, 1995); it is a product of market forces and needs the market to sustain economic viability. Independent consultants are mainly accountable through consumer purchase, and the operation of such a process means that the percieved and constructed needs of the consumer dominate. If a school is about to be 'OFSTEDed' and rings you up for a consultancy to prepare the staff, it is a foolish consultant who refuses a day's training on efficiency and effectiveness and tries to persuade the school that what they really need is a day on the theory of how children learn. Consultants have recognized quite quickly that their professional knowledge as relevant and recent practice is soon dated and so becomes irrelevant to the world of management. Therefore in order to survive within a competitive marketplace there are pressures to embrace the 'quick fix approach'. Even the recognition of values and ethics is insufficient to ensure that the widespread and unreflexive promotion of business models and techniques is halted. Furthermore, it is a delusion to argue that if teachers grasp the reforms and make them work for them they can resist the worst excesses of managerialism. The Education Management Industry characterizes managerialism as 'management for its own sake where systems, status and routines take priority over real needs' (West-Burnham, 1992, p.9) rather than understanding that managerialism is about controlling how needs are identified. There is a clear failure within the Education Management Industry and within the field of education management as a whole to engage in a reflective and reflexive process on what the purpose of education management is, and why this growth of 'management by ringbinder' has taken place.

The Education Management Industry and the reflective practitioner

The growth of the Education Management Industry is part of a wider perspective and we need to consider the transformation in the lives and work of teachers. Teachers looked for support at a time when their concept of being a professional was coming under very serious attack. We are all familiar with the critique of teachers and teaching as:

- promoting their own self-interest or 'a form of conspiracy against the public' (Strain, 1995, p.41);
- defending the bureaucratic state as an educational monopoly against the consumer rights and choices of the active citizen;
- promoting a curriculum that expanded beyond what could reasonably be afforded and bore little relationship with what the economy demanded.

Ball (1990a) has shown how the ideology of the New Right through 'discourses of derision' constructed education policy in which 'producers' such as teachers were marginalized in favour of the 'consumers' (i.e. parents and industrialists). Furthermore, the claims by teachers to be professionals fell on deaf ears, and as Ozga (1995) has shown, the manipulation of the reality and rhetoric of teacher professionalism is linked to state control. The growth in teacher autonomy ensured a division between teachers and parents, and as Ozga (1995) states:

> That division permitted the co-option of parents into a new 'partnership' for the 'reform' of the education system. The capacity of teachers to resist such initiatives was weakened by the failure of education policy designed to eradicate inequality; it was becoming apparent to teachers that education could not, after all, compensate for society. Furthermore, teachers were having to cope with a simultaneous decline in both resources and pupil numbers. All these factors combined to create favourable circumstances for the reassertion of control over teachers in England. (p.27)

What is interesting when pursuing a historical approach is that the Education Management Industry has clearly colluded with this control over the teaching profession. What does being a professional mean? In the world of the educational management product the teacher should not claim to have power and a status exclusive from the consumer whose needs are paramount and define quality; and the teacher should not claim exclusivity in knowledge and skills, and certainly ought to look at outcomes and the efficiency of processes that deliver them. Rather, the courses, books and packages about management knowledge and competences mean that the teacher becomes a better professional with open and measurable skills delivering measurable outcomes in a responsive and consumer-driven way. Therefore, instead of claiming to have esoteric and intangible professional rights to be hidden from the gaze of the suffering taxpayer, the teacher as manager can proudly claim to be the same as the parent working in the private sector. As Busher and Saran (1995) have confidently stated,

> In the ... partnership paradigm, ironically perhaps, teachers are once again trusted professionals who are believed by the community to know how to construct a high-quality school experience with and for the students. But in this case it is because there is an open and honest dialogue between teachers and the community about how education is undertaken – not, as formerly, because of teachers' claims to a great and mysterious expertise. Promoting such a dialogue may involve schools and teachers using a range of marketing techniques, not as glib sales devices, but to research how best a school can begin to meet the educational wants and needs which its students and potential students and their parents have. (p.202)

Within the education management product, human resource management dominates, with teachers being reprofessionalized through teams, exercising leadership, participating in decision-making, being empowered, valufacturing (de Bond, 1993) and living the vision. What is missing within these products is a real understanding of the historical and theoretical framework in which they are being produced and packaged. For example, we have seen that teaching skills have been reduced to a series of identifiable competences that can be assessed and this has been complemented by managerial competences. A teacher will begin, proceed and complete their career within an externally defined framework that has not been created out of thin air, but is part of a means of controlling teachers (Jones and Moore, 1993). Ball (1990b) has shown that management is a discourse as well as a professional ideology in which there is a separate language, defined skills and knowledge for an elite of managers within schools. It is within this context that we need to view Headlamp and other competency-driven accreditation and training initiatives. In an ever turbulent world the key aim of the manager is to bring order and control through the exercise of rational processes. What the rapid adoption of the managerial model has done is to exclude other versions of organization life from teacher training and development. Management is an ideology and is central to the New Right policies and legislation that has been transforming teacher's work and their relationships.

What is the impact on the sense of teacher professionalism? Clearly, in order to promote the managerial model a number of critiques have been prevalent. Firstly, teacher autonomy has been ridiculed as preventing collegiality, and managerial skills and processes enable teachers to work in teams on the basis of consensus value systems. However, as Sparkes and Bloomer (1993) have argued,

> collegial support and partnership cannot be mandated. Indeed, the notions of collegiality and partnership are themselves socially constructed and negotiated in the working context of the school day that is permeated by power relationships. (p.177)

When this is put within the education policy context then, as Hargreaves (1994) has identified, there is a 'contrived collegiality' which wastes valuable expertise and skills, and is evident,

> when spontaneous, dangerous and difficult-to-control forms of teacher collaboration are discouraged or usurped by administrators who capture it, contain it and contrive it through compulsory cooperation, required collaborative planning, stage-managed mission statements, labyrinthine procedures of school development planning, and processes of collaboration to implement non-negotiable programs and curricula whose viability and practicality are not open to discussion. (p.80)

Secondly, professional judgement and standards have been questioned by the adoption of external critieria in assessment and the marginalization of the teacher in relation to the curriculum. Therefore, children's work is determined by efficiency rather than welfare, and they are tested according to a timetable rather than readiness and capability. Ball (1990a) has argued that the teacher has become a technician delivering the curriculum:

> ERA is not just about control over the definition of school knowledge. It is also about control over teachers and teachers' work. It rests upon a profound distrust of teachers and seeks to close down many of the areas of discretion previously available to them. (p.214)

Therefore, the knowledge and skills rooted in professionalism have been set aside by the discourse of the need to learn 'new' and external skills. What teachers have always known about the importance of values and radicalism, of the realism of micropolitics and the personal investment in human relationships is not regarded as useful in a world of efficiency and accountability. This is nowhere better illustrated than by the concept of the Reflective Practitioner and how it is used within the Education Management Industry. Central to courses, books and other products is the manager as problem-solver in which there is an emphasis on decision-making in relation to outcomes, process and content: what do we want to achieve, in what way, and what information and skills do we need to do it? In this sense we can reflect while doing it: by reflection-on-practice and reflection-in-practice, or we can be proactive by reflection-for-practice (Schon, 1983). This is a theory of action which is valuable to the teacher and to the manager, but it will remain shallow unless it is (a) seen within the policy context, and (b) rooted in knowledge creation. Smyth (1992), citing O'Connor (1984), has argued that advocating that the teacher should 'reflect on the practical' must be seen in relation to the policy context, and in particular to the crisis within the state and the contradictory tensions between capital accumulation and democratic legitimation:

> ... the desire of the state, on the one hand, to promote the infrastructure and climate necessary to reproduce labor power of the right kind to serve the requirements of capital and, on the other hand, the devising of ways to maximize and maintain mass support, particularly in terms of the flexibility, creativity, and understanding that workers bring to the work process. (p.276)

Therefore restructuring has enabled centralization to increase with control over the educational product and at the same time manage the reduction in public sector resources for education through the decentralization of budgetary responsibility. As Smyth (1992) goes on to say:

> The reality, therefore, is that such local initiatives do not amount to a redistribution of power, but rather they constitute limited discretionary control over the implementation of decisions and directions determined centrally by others, not an active process of contesting, debating, and determining the nature of those ends. (p.280)

So, what is this empowerment that dominates education management products? Does being empowered really mean that the school can reject established practice and exercise choice in the way that Hargreaves and Hopkins (1991) identify?

> Management is, as the textbooks tell us, about structures and procedures. However, because these have often evolved over time, they are taken for granted and regarded as fixed and immutable. We prefer the term *management arrangements*. This emphasizes that the content of management is a set of arrangements which are *chosen* by the members of an organization to help them to conduct their affairs and realize their aims. Because they are chosen, from a wide variety of possible arrangements, they can be changed or adapted according to circumstances and preferences. (p.15)

Or is it that empowerment is not really about real choice but is an illusion created by popular discourses that are legitimizing New Right policies? Troyna (1994a) has used the work of Edelman (1964, 1977) to show that empowerment is 'part of the "symbolic political language" of the current educational reforms and functions as one of the key "condensation symbols" in policy discourse' (p.79). Therefore empowerment has been created and is used

> to create symbolic stereotypes and metaphors which reassure supporters that their interests have been considered. But they are framed in ways that the proposed solutions may also be contradictory or ambiguously related to the way supporters originally viewed the issue.   (Troyna, 1994a, p.73)

In other words, empowerment promises a new professionalism of collegiality and consensus, but at the same time there is sufficient ambiguity in the tension between being given a voice and actually having the real authority to make a difference, that control remains firmly centralized both locally within the school hierarchies and externally within Whitehall and its numerous quangos.

Central to this is the issue of knowledge creation and the role of the reflective practitioner within it. This is the Education Management Industry's Achilles heel, as through its proformas, checklists and top tips it does not facilitate the development of knowledge necessary for the truly reflective practitioner. For example, the in-service trainer may present the teacher with the 'no time for management' problem. That is, you are too busy doing 'it' to stand back and think about how you might do 'it' better, especially by the adoption of management strategies such as auditing, deploying and evaluating time spent. If teachers present different interpretations of what 'it' is by reflecting on what their purpose is, then a rejection of managerial consensus building is often characterized as a rejection of the language of management. In other words, teachers are cynical of 'audits' and 'ownership', and therefore the trainer's function is to get across the underlying techniques of management without letting technical words get in the way. However, the promotion of management strategies cuts the teacher off from a more in-depth process of knowledge creation. Shulman (1987) has argued that there are seven broad categories of knowledge for successful reflection by the teacher:

- content knowledge;
- general pedagogical knowledge, with special reference to those broad principles and strategies of classroom management and organization that appear to transcend the subject matter;
- curriculum knowledge, with particular grasp of the materials and programs that serve as "tools of the trade" for teachers;
- pedagogical content knowledge, that special amalgam of content and pedagogy that is uniquely the province of teachers, their own special form of professional understanding;
- knowledge of learners and their characteristics;
- knowledge of educational contexts, ranging from the workings of the group or classroom, the governance and financing of school districts, to the character of communities and cultures; and
- knowledge of educational ends, purposes, and values, and their philosophical and historical grounds. (p.8)

However, there is little of this evident within education management products and they put their emphasis outside of the classroom, and the key words are accountability and quality, rather than about pedagogic processes. Children and students do not figure in these products except as resources or as consumers. Furthermore, a teacher with a knowledge of educational policy, who has read Bourdieu or Foucault, is a dangerous person to have on an in-service course as they will be a different type of reflective practitioner. Teachers who read and think are dangerous within the world of management because they have emancipatory knowledge developed through the reflexive process. As Elliott (1991) has argued:

> Reflective practice implies reflexivity: self-awareness. But such an awareness brings with it insights into the ways in which the self in action is shaped and constrained by institutional structures. Self awareness and awareness of the institutional context of one's work as a teacher are not developed by separate cognitive processes: reflexive and object analysis. They are qualities of the same reflexive process. Reflexive practice necessarily implies both self-critique and institutional critique. One cannot have one without the other. (p.38)

Education management puts a lot of emphasis on self-critique, in which the practitioner is invited to confess through self-review and appraisal in order to obtain a fit with the consensus value system, or leave. There is also an encouragement of institutional critique through challenging what are conceptualized as limitations to effective and efficient management, such as teacher autonomy and trade unions. Beyond this, education management products cannot go, as they are concerned with achieving stability, organizational fit and consensus. Therefore, the true reflective practitioner (or perhaps reflective professional) so evident within the literature has been lost, and can be defined as one who engages in political action. As Kemmis (1991) has argued, teachers who engage in emancipatory action research

> demonstrate that they can find new and what they themselves regard as better ways to interpret their own educational action in context, and new ways to act in the practical, political circumstances of schooling in which they find themselves. (p.63)

We would have to search long and hard to find the real reflective practitioner being developed in management in-service courses and checklists. What seems to be the case is that the label 'reflective practitioner' is often added to engender legitimacy, and in relation to practice the in-service process does allow for the participant to think and discuss. However, the urgency and correctness of the management imperative means that reflection takes place within a given framework of certain values, knowledge and skills. For example, education management products dealing with professional development emphasize the importance of reflection as a collaborative activity. I cannot argue with that, except the type of collaboration put forward is about having critical friends, mentors, an appraiser or a personal development profile. Problem-solving requires smooth and tidy processes in which values have to be managed. As Inglis (1985) has shown:

> Management becomes the refinement of techniques for ensuring complicity in its systemic ends ... Counselling, a process in education reserved for those who in one way or another have been chewed up and spat out by the system, becomes the administration of similar techniques which console or in other ways (at times pharmacological) sedate the victim over his or her anti-socially lived disappointment ... It is your business, as both manager and counsellor, to persuade those who disagree to see reason, but reason then turns out to mean the reasonableness of giving way to superior power. (p.102)

The industry is about controlling teachers and making them compliant with the external policy context, because a fundamental aim of managerialism is to depoliticize organizational behaviour. Clarke *et al.* (1994) show the irony within this, as professionalism and bureaucracy were promoted within the public sector in the 1960s and 1970s as enabling the creation of neutral structures and the application of expert knowledge through which issues could be debated. However, the managerialist project has been about characterizing this as enabling the creation of partisan and privileged groups who block change, and therefore the efficiency and effectiveness of managerialism is presented as neutralizing. We are never invited to ask: who wants me to be efficient and why? The Education Management Industry is unable to give recognition to this as it lacks authentic historical and theoretical approaches to explain teacher professionalism and what is really happening to teachers' lives and work.

Summary

There are a number of excellent scholarly textbooks and articles that have charted and explained in different ways what has happened to teachers' lives and the changing control over their work, such as Apple (1989), Ball (1987, 1990a, 1993), Hargreaves (1984), Hatcher (1994), Ozga and Lawn (1988). In these types of writing we are able to gain access to historical and theoretical analyses of, for example, how teacher professionalism can be seen in relation to ideology (Strain, 1995) or occupational restructuring by the state (Ozga, 1995). Furthermore, there is a growing critique of the managerialist state (Clarke *et al.*, 1994; Clarke and Stewart, 1992; Farnham and Horton, 1992a, 1992b; Pollitt, 1990; Stewart and Walsh, 1992), which prompts us to ask how and why have teachers found themselves in a context in which 'employees are promised a more "people-centred" working environment (or the chance to keep their jobs) in return for doing "more for less"' (Clarke *et al.*, 1994, p.239).

The Education Management Industry proceeds in spite of this work and we are left asking: does the Industry look at its role in working with teachers? Its role in knowledge production? Its role in the changing power structures within the education system? Its role in the policy implementation process? This book is not a cynical attempt to put education management in the dock: it is already there! Unfortunately, there is little evidence within the education management products that this is recognized and understood. A case is being made which sees education management as a part of the macropolitical project of the New Right in its attempts to neutralize the micropolitical activities of educational professionals. The Education Management Industry is not being accused of a collaborative conspiracy, but of an unreflective and unreflexive collusion with the managerialist project.

The challenge for the Education Management Industry presented within this book is to engage in the type of reflective practitioner processes that are denied within education management products: a political actor rather than a fraternizer. Chapter 2 presents an opportunity to do just that by engaging in a reflective and reflexive approach through the use of the Jurassic Management metaphor, and by focusing on self-management products. Chapter 3 is concerned with exploring the role of theory in education management products, and argues that the managerialist agenda is focused more on perpetuating ignorance than on knowledge creation. Chapter 4 goes on to consider the absence of historical analysis within education management products and the consequent impact on research design. Chapter 5 provides the opportunity for participants in the Education Management Industry to consider the scientific foundations of the management strategies in 'management-by-ringbinder' products. The book concludes with Chapter 6, which invites consideration of the critical choices for the education management in the creation of the future.

We may ask: why such a critique and why now? As I have said earlier, this is a product of personal experiences as an observer, as both a teacher and a lecturer in education management. My first degree is in modern history and politics and therefore I bring to my critique issues to do with historical analysis and political science theory and concepts. This is timely, as books and articles are being published in which a critique is growing (Angus, 1994; Ball, 1990b; Hatcher, 1994; Ozga, 1992; and Smyth, 1993), and the rise of Education Policy Sociology means that education management not only has to come to terms with this type of analysis but also to use it as an opportunity to reflect on its own purpose. At the moment there is very little reflection and reflexivity about education management (Bottery (1992) and Davies (1990) stand out), and if there is to be a meaningful debate about management in education then it should not be one-sided and education management participants are entitled to be a part of it.

CHAPTER 2

A metaphor

Michael Crichton's (1991) *Jurassic Park* is not only a bestseller and box-office hit but is also a metaphor for describing and understanding management development for educational professionals. Jurassic Park is the world's ultimate theme park and the connection may not be immediately obvious, but if the story is studied in detail then fiction becomes fact when the values and strategies underpinning this entertainment project are compared with what is being promoted as effective management in schools and colleges.

The fictional Jurassic Park failed because the senior management thought that a right-to-manage strategy combined with skilful marketing would bring success. For those delivering and experiencing in-service training and management development for the self-managing school/college, the alarm bells should be ringing. A reflexive and reflective approach within the Education Management Industry would enable questions to be asked about whether we are seducing managers into adopting strategies that will lead to failure or whether we are effectively training managers with the necessary knowledge to create a future for our schools and colleges.

Identifying Jurassic management

John Hammond, the visionary of the Isla Nublar entertainment theme park, has conceptualized his vision and mission as a linear systems strategy, which is illustrated in Figure 2.1. This model enables the vision to be output-led rather than input-driven. As Hammond states:

> ... the concept of the most advanced amusement park in the world, combining the latest electronic and biological technologies. I'm not talking about *rides*. Everybody has *rides*. Coney island has rides ... So we set out to make biological attractions. *Living* attractions. Attractions so astonishing they would capture the imagination of the entire world. (Crichton, 1991, p.62)

This entrepreneurial spirit is evident in the prediction of huge profits from entertaining the super-rich, plus the income generation from

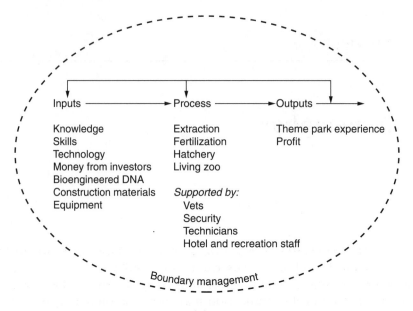

Inputs   → Process   →Outputs

Knowledge   Extraction   Theme park experience
Skills   Fertilization   Profit
Technology   Hatchery
Money from investors   Living zoo
Bioengineered DNA
Construction materials   *Supported by:*
Equipment   Vets
                           Security
                           Technicians
                           Hotel and recreation staff

Boundary management

Figure 2.1. Jurassic management systems model

merchandising. In response to the question 'What is the biological equivalent of a Sony Walkman?' (Crichton, 1991, p.66), the answer is to identify a perceived demand for 'consumer biologicals', and therefore tourists will leave the island with not only T-shirts but also their own patented pet dinosaur.

The input–process–output system enables current management thinking to be implemented. Expert boundary scanning and analysis has taken place, and Hammond has completed a Political, Economic, Social and Technological (PEST) analysis to identify where the theme park lies on the closed–open system continuum. There is a commitment to be 'close to the customer' (Peters and Waterman, 1982, p.156) and a drive to ensure that the organization achieves 'a fit between its customer requirements and its own capabilities' (Stacey, 1991, p.115). Quality means conformance to customer requirements and Hammond has a clear understanding of customer expectations. An information blackout on the project means that a spectacular opening will ensure the ultimate in 'delighting the customer' (Peters, 1988, p.92).

However, Hammond is mindful of the need to control the boundaries, and the theme park has been designed to withstand shocks from the environment and therefore ensure stability. Within the island there are closed boundaries, such as the use of fences and moats, and biological limits, such as all the dinosaurs are female, sterile and dependent on the amino acid lysine. Within the compounds there is computer tracking, and as a backup there are defence systems and weapons. The relationship between Jurassic Park and the outside world has been carefully thought out, and the key emphasis is on equilibrium. The ability of the organization to manage its boundaries is guaranteed by geographic isolation, controlled transport into and out of the island, a high price tag for visitors, the sanctity of private property, frontiers of knowledge that are in the commercial company rather than the university, and independence from the interference of the laws of the developed world.

The quality management processes operating within the theme park are central to the success of the project. Hammond has undertaken a SWOT (Strengths, Weaknesses, Opportunties and Threats) analysis on the theme park project. The strengths are in the value-added concept in which the past is reconstructed with real dinosaurs and niche marketed to the right client base. Anticipated weaknesses have been eradicated by proactive strategic planning and state-of-the-art computer and information systems. There will be no need to downsize in this operation; the inputs will be processed by small dedicated teams of staff comprised of scientists, information systems managers, food handlers and clean-up crews, who will operate within a 'hands on, value-driven' culture (Peters and Waterman, 1982, p.279). By conceptualizing the staff as a human resource, the theme park is organizationally fit and capable of meeting customer requirements (Oakland, 1989, p.3). Furthermore, by 'sticking to the knitting' (Peters and Waterman, 1982, p.292) cause and effect are close and directly connected. Therefore Hammond may have been mindful of his success indicators and time targets when he states:

> I tell you that everything on the island is going forward as planned. Everything on that island is perfectly *fine*.   (Crichton, 1991, p.63)

This high degree of certainty, and with it the predictive ability of linear systems, is rooted in Newtonian physics. For Hammond, knowledge comes from 'keeping track of things' (Crichton, 1991, p.160) in order to be proactive and prevent crisis management. Critical to the success of Jurassic Park is Hammond's leadership and his 'bias for action' (Peters and Waterman, 1982, p.119). He has clearly been on a management development training course or even had his competences assessed. Hammond has marketed his reputation so well that he is considered as being 'about as sinister as Walt Disney' (Crichton, 1991, p.43). His values are explicit: he knows the type of business that he is in, and how that business should be run. Hammond has appointed and trained winners (Blanchard and Johnson, 1983) who are focused on the common purpose of profit and entertainment. For Hammond his judgement is sound, he knows when and how to listen, and also when to make the key decisions.

Given that the management philosophy underlying Jurassic Park is based on much of the current writings on what makes a successful organization, we may well ask: what went wrong? Has Hammond's MBA let him down? The next section will consider the dominance of Hammond's Jurassic Management approach and raise questions that current management orthodoxy cannot answer.

Jurassic management: a lost world

Current writers in both business and education management would find much in Jurassic Management to approve of: the concept of a common purpose with benchmarking and success indicators; teams empowered to live the vision based on a consensus value system; planning and organizational effectiveness; a skilled marketing strategy based on sound boundary management; and meeting the needs of the customer by adapting to the environment (Stacey, 1991). Within education the development of the self-managing and self-governing educational institution in the form of the local management of schools (LMS), grant-maintained status (GMS) and Incorporation, has led managers to rush to take training courses on strategic and human resource management to ensure survival in the new educational marketplace. The business culture has rapidly been imposed on educational institutions, and entrepreneurial processes are being promoted as the solution to managing open-ended change in a turbulent environment.

However, we need to take care. While the *Jurassic Park* metaphor is interesting and illuminating, it could be argued that the failure of Jurassic Park is due to the sediments in Hammond's management style and process from an earlier age of bureaucracy and transactional leadership (Johnson and Gill, 1993). However, even if Hammond had an MBA with a distinction, Jurassic Park would still fail because of the fundamental flaw in current management training: to know the future! (Stacey, 1992). This vital observation will be illustrated by examining concerns about visioning, structure, boundary management and planning.

Management writers could argue that Hammond does not understand the visioning process and certainly cannot handle revisiting the vision, and sees raising questions as threatening rather than creative. Therefore, Hammond has failed to understand that successful action is by short steps rather than by giant leaps. Management writers have argued that this trial and error approach is vital because, 'if the specific outcomes of actions are unknown, dramatic failure of one action could be a terminal matter for the organization' (Stacey, 1992, p.117). Hence Jurassic Park fails because of one action: the acceleration of the dinosaur programme before information, as opposed to assumptions, about the current dinosaurs has been gathered.

Perhaps we should not be asking what is wrong with Hammond's visioning process, but what is wrong with visioning itself. Visioning seems to have been the solution to a rejection of mechanistic, scientific and bureaucratic models. Due to turbulent change we cannot operate management by objectives, but we can have a vision of a future state that we can move towards. However, the assumptions on which the vision is based could be wrong, and therefore the real reason Jurassic Park failed is because:

> ... one of the core beliefs of the planners ... (was that) ... the animals, however exotic, would fundamentally behave like animals in zoos anywhere. They would

learn the regularities of their care, and they would respond.

(Crichton, 1991, p.141)

The values on which the assumptions are based may not be shared and therefore there could be conflicts over whether genetic engineering should be used for 'entertainment' or for 'medical advances'. Even if there is agreement on the vision of 'entertainment' and the ultimate theme park, there is a lack of clarity between Hammond and his chief scientist as to whether the dinosaurs should be seen (or not seen) in a replicated reality, or whether the dinosaurs should be genetically engineered not to run so fast and so be accessible to the paying customer. We therefore need to consider whether visioning is not only an illusion but a delusion, in that it seduces managers into planning and organizing in order to control the future rather than utilizing strategies to create it (Stacey, 1993).

The management structure of Jurassic Park may be leaner but it is not flatter! Management writers would argue that Hammond sensibly retains financial control, but there is still a hierarchy and there is no effective strategy for empowering teams. Jurassic 'teams' are really groups of people who are specialists in the same area, and the size and composition of the 'teams' is based on economy rather than effectiveness. The culture in which the 'teams' work is uncreative in that failure is failure rather than something to learn from, and therefore it is only to be expected that there will be disgruntled employees who will sell the company secrets to a rival.

However, we should not be asking what is wrong with Hammond's failure in human resource management, but whether teams and value-driven organizations really are the solution to the fact that management is messy and has to deal with ambiguity and paradox. The language of empowerment and ownership may be used and heard, but in fact proactively created teams mean that participation is 'in the gift of management' (Bottery, 1992, p.163) and therefore control shifts from being a bureaucratic process to being a human resource process. The capacity for human beings to self-organize around issues and form political interest groups is underestimated and underutilized. The emphasis on rational team decision-making fails to allow for how adults really do learn and the importance of 'reasoning by analogy' (Stacey, 1991, p.166). Furthermore, we need to consider whether teams based on consensus value systems only give recognition to organizationally defined skills and do not recognize the plurality of skills that people have.

Management writers would argue that Hammond failed to manage his boundaries and hence Jurassic Park was destabilized. However, we should not be focusing our attention on a lack of perceived skill, but whether organizations should seek stability with their environment or recognize that they create their environment. Therefore, we need to consider whether an organization trying to achieve a stable equilibrium with the environment by meeting client needs is uncreative. Could it be the case that managers who vision, plan and engage in market research will not be innovative and fail to manage change?

Poor boundary management could be interpreted by management writers as being the cause of the failure of Hammond's planning process in that the required information needed to review, forecast, prioritize and implement is missing. However, we should not be criticizing the niceties of Hammond's institutional development plan, but questioning whether long-term forecasting and planning should take place. Stacey (1992) has asked whether we can say anything useful about the future, and therefore we need to consider whether linearity (input–process–output) is a distortion and should not be applied to organizations. This is illustrated by one of Crichton's (1991) characters:

> Straight linearity, which we have come to take for granted in everything from physics to fiction, simply does not exist. Linearity is an artificial way of viewing the world. Real life isn't a series of interconnected events occurring one after another ... life is actually a series of encounters in which one event may change those that follow in a wholly unpredictable, even devastating way. (p.172)

Living systems are inherently unpredictable and therefore the emphasis should not be on organizational goals but on the critical choices that managers have to make at different times in the life of the organization. Feedback into the system from both quantitative and qualitative indicators is critical because small changes can have huge effects.

Jurassic management: an undiscovered world

There are much deeper concerns than the ones identified above and they can be illustrated by using the purpose of this book as an analogy. If this book's purpose was to problem-solve then the approach now would be to take each of the concerns raised about management and provide strategies to enable the effective and efficient manager to move forward. I cannot do this. Jurassic Park failed not just because there are problems in visioning, strategic management, structure and boundary scanning, but because Hammond (like all applied managerialists) fails to give recognition to the knowledge base on which his project is founded. We need to ask questions not just about what, but about the why and how:

- How is history investigated and used, and why?
- How is theory developed and used, and why?
- How is research undertaken and used, and why?

There is no history in Jurassic Park. While the dinosaur and entertainment experience is replicated pre-history, the actual vision and mission of the project is based literally on an island in the clouds. Competences are organizationally defined and there is no recognition of the knowledge, skills and understanding that all workers bring with them to the island (though events do show how history provides a counter culture to the consensus-building approach). The structural injustices of the outside world cannot have an impact on the project: there is no racisim, sexism or ageism on Isla Nublar because organizational behaviour is focused purely on income generation as a higher form of human activity and motivation. Furthermore, there is no sense of Hammond ever having explored the concept of a utopia, either philosophically or historically, by studying examples of communities brought together around a specific project and set of values. The impression given is that if Jurassic Park was closed down as a failing theme park then all that would be needed to reopen it within a few months is refurbishment, a new staff appointed and new dinosaurs hatched. Hammond has plans to set up Jurassic Parks in Europe and Asia irrespective of their histories and cultural traditions.

Research in Jurassic Park is essentially 'contractual': the scientists have undertaken the necessary biological research to create and sustain the product that the InGen company has funded. As Crichton (1991) has argued:

> ... the attitude of pure scientists was fundamentally critical toward the work of applied scientists, and to industry in general. Their longstanding antagonism kept university scientists free of contaminating industry ties, and whenever debate arose about technological matters, disinterested scientists were available to discuss the issues at the highest levels.
>
> But that is no longer true. There are very few molecular biologists and very few research institutions without commerical affiliations. The old days are gone. Genetic research continues, at a more furious pace than ever. But it is done in secret, and in haste, and for profit. (Crichton, 1991, p.xi)

The consequences of this are played out in Jurassic Park, and are illustrated by Hammond, who, as the entrepreneur, defines research questions in order to solve real and tangible problems. Knowledge is therefore about enabling, doing, achieving and performing. As Hammond states:

> Universities are no longer the intellectual centers of the country. The very idea is preposterous. Universities are the backwater ... Universities simply aren't where it's happening any more. And they haven't been for forty years. If you want to do something important in computers or genetics, you don't go to a *university*. (p.125)

There is a sense here that there is useful and there is useless knowledge, and clearly it is knowledge that is generated within an entrepreneurial problem-solving setting and value system which is *useful*. Hammond is investing in entertainment because, 'nobody needs entertainment' (Crichton, 1991, p.199) and therefore nobody interferes. Hammond contrasts this with drugs research:

> Sick people aren't going to pay a thousand dollars a dose for needed medication – they won't be grateful, they'll be outraged. Blue Cross isn't going to pay it. They'll scream highway robbery. So something will happen. Your patent application will be denied. Your permits will be delayed. *Something* will force you to see reason – and to sell your drug at a lower cost. From a business standpoint, that makes helping mankind a very risky business. Personally, I would *never* help mankind. (p.199)

Hammond's strategic approach to product development is based on certainty, predictability, rationality and control. This is presented as common sense and for Hammond it has clearly been internalized and become intuitive: there is nothing so practical as a good theory. It is left to others in the story to show its roots in Newtonian science of three hundred years ago, and to acknowledge that there have been paradigm shifts in science such as Chaos Theory, in which human and social interactions can be described, and more importantly, explained in a very different way.

Jurassic education management

A recent advertisement for a headteacher in *The Times Educational Supplement* states:

> The successful applicant will be committed to the mission statement, possess a sound knowledge of current educational issues, collaborative management skills and the energy and vision to lead the school community into the 21st Century   (*TES*, 1 January 1995)

Jurassic Management is clearly having an impact (if only on the language used in job advertisements and descriptions!) on those responsible for the governance of schools. The models promoted by management writers are very seductive for education managers facing the restructuring of the system in relation to: curriculum; teaching and learning; funding and income generation; staffing and conditions of service; and governance. The solution put forward in the 'how-to-do-it' education management texts and manuals, by government agencies and by training packages is to take on the management philosophy of Jurassic Park. Managers of schools and colleges who are facing the challenges of a competitive business market are seeking stability, reciprocity, consensus and consistency, and are therefore engaging in the following:

(1) Visioning and the formulation of mission statements.
(2) Institutional development planning with processes involving review, forecasting, implementation and evaluation.
(3) Niche marketing to current and potential clients supported by boundary scanning and market research with pupil/student, parental and staff surveys.
(4) Maximizing inputs in relation to open enrolment, formula funding and income generation by full cost courses and bidding for contracts (e.g. from the new Teacher Training Agency).
(5) Teams operate in a task culture based on accepted and common values. Skills are organizationally defined and are rewarded according to performance appraisal systems.
(6) Outputs are concerned with measuring the quantitative and qualitative indicators in relation to value added.
(7) Information management is being used to control behaviour as

dinosaur tracking is replaced by student tracking using smart cards.

(8) Inspection by government agencies (OFSTED, FEFC, HEFC) is based on accountability for the application of business and human resource management processes in enabling effective and efficient teaching and learning.

At this point we can ask the question: can the current philosophy behind management training enable schools and colleges to be successful within a rapidly changing environment? According to the vast array of education management products then the answer to that question is yes. However, what the Jurassic Management metaphor allows us to do is to raise doubts in a field of study and application which is so characterized by certainty. This has the potential to put those working in the Education Management Industry in contact with the call for revisionism.

Doubts and concerns about the Education Management Industry and its impact on schools can be illustrated by looking at the self-managing school staffed by self-managing individuals. The debate about the self-managing school has focused on the work of writers such as Caldwell and Spinks (1988), who have argued that leadership is about vision and

> the importance of the leader gaining the commitment of others to that vision and then ensuring that it shapes the policies, plans and day-to-day activities ... (p.174)

The strategy of Collaborative Management, as put forward by Caldwell and Spinks, is rooted in the work of Peters and Waterman (1982), and has been criticized for legitimizing the policies of the New Right as well as training managers to lead their schools and colleges into decline. In the world of the self-managing school, complexity is marginalized and management is unproblematic and tidy (Ball, 1993). Managers need not fear, because if they understand the ingredients and follow the method, the recipe will not let them down. Angus (1993, 1994) has provided a thorough critique of the self-managing school: firstly, there is an 'uncritical acceptance' of Thatcherite policies in which the 1987 Conservative election manifesto is presented as uncontroversial, and key concepts such as choice and equity are not analysed within the policy changes advocated (1994, p.82). Secondly, the conceptualization of the school as a neutral place where problem-solving takes place by the employment of the correct management techniques means that it is

> an unreal world that is remote from social relations of inequality, cultural hege-mony, sexism, racism or any of the social and educational disadvantages and conflicts that surround and pervade schooling. (1993, p.22)

Consider the question: what is the purpose of education? This is never asked within education management products because this type of question is too complex and requires analysis, which prevents the problem-solving agenda from operating. Thirdly, the rhetoric o the self-managing school is one of delegation, empowerment, leadership ¿nd participation, in which the teacher as manager is celebrated above the teacher as pedagogic professional. The actual reality of teaching and managing a school in the 1990s is therefore obscured, and it redirects the blame for resource limits to the financial management processes of the school rather than the structural economic injustices in which the school is operating. There is no room in the self-managing school for ethnographic research into the real lives and experiences of teachers, rather the internal research processes are based on rational and objective procedures for auditing and the gathering of data for management decision-making.

What 'management by ringbinder' is doing is forcing managers to transfer the strategies used to control the predictable short-term to the unknowable long-term (Stacey, 1992). Managers like the visioning and human resource management processes because they enable them to deal with their fear of not being in control by promoting an illusion of the future supported by sham participation (Anderson and Dixon, 1993). What educational managers may not have realized is that the rapid adoption of Jurassic Management strategies has meant that schools and colleges have been able to collaborate with the very policies that have created the fear. Furthermore, just as burglar alarm companies create a climate of fear and then provide solutions in the form of boundary management, then so does Jurassic Management training. Making households the problem in relation to crime deflects attention away from the real problem of appropriate social and economic policies. Installing a burglar alarm could literally lure the household into a false sense of security by creating a feeling of safety in the midst of turmoil, rather than encouraging contributions to the debate about the causes of the turmoil.

The impact of managerialist models on the teacher is under-researched in the field of education management and it is highly unlikely that a handbook on an aspect of problem-solving in a school would contain a Professional Health Warning to the effect: this handbook is designed to turn all teachers into 'technicians' (Ball, 1990a); or, this handbook is designed to ensure teacher compliance (Hatcher, 1994). Callahan's (1962) work on the USA education system led to the development of the 'vulnerability thesis' in which the demand for efficiency in the first three decades of this century made educational administrators/managers vulnerable to hostile public opinion and questions about purpose and outcomes at a time of growing job insecurity. The higher education market responded to this through the provision of training and accreditation. In recent years educational professionals have been equally vulnerable in England and Wales in both the identification and provision of management training and current trends in what makes the teacher an effective and efficient professional are firmly rooted in business models such as Total Quality Management, and Investors in People. In the last ten years there has been a growth in the number of self-management products: books, tapes, videos and training courses. There is a wide range of books that give the reader the opportunity to engage in interactive and therapeutic processes by purchasing packages such as Nicholson (1992), Pedlar and Boydell (1985), Pedlar *et al.* (1994) and Trotter (1993). These products tend to be generic, and, with the exception of Trotter (1993), are not focused on the education setting. However, these and other publications are quoted and used widely in dedicated education management products. The general theme is based on the premise of the need to manage self before managing others, and as Pedlar *et al.* (1994) point out:

> Self development is personal development, with the person taking primary responsibility for her or his own learning and for choosing the means to achieve this. (p.5)

In other words, the importance of self-management is seen in relation to developing a sense of personal worth and self-esteem, and this enables the development of specific qualities and skills which will release unrealized potential and lead to personal fulfilment, and improve job performance and advancement. This is facilitated by being able to participate in tasks that tend to be based on the model in Table 2.1.

Table 2.1. The self-management process: the individual agenda

Stage in process	Questions to ask of yourself
Awareness	Why is self-management an issue for me?
Self-audit	Where am I now?
Goal-setting	Where do I want to be? What are my learning needs? What are my priorities?
Identifying the gap	How do I get there? What are my options?
Closing the gap	What techniques do I need to work on? How will I monitor my progress? Who can I count on to help me? How will I know when I have achieved an objective?

This process is made manageable by the design of the materials, so that

> you can work on some of the exercises a bit at a time, using odd half hours on train journeys, between meetings, in the bath, or in bed if you are keen enough. Some of the activities need to be tackled at work, such as observing how meetings work and trying out different forms of personal investigation. Others you can work through in informal contact with colleagues, over lunch for instance, to test their perceptions against your own.   (Pedlar, 1994, p.7)

The materials tend to be proformas, self-evaluating questionnaires, simple models to hold in the head, and quotations or soundbites that have a clear but profound message. On the surface these materials may look trivial, but it is how they are managed within the context of the written/multimedia package or within an in-service session that is important: the simplest ideas can be very powerful for the individual. What all these materials have in common is the need to involve the participant by interacting, and then encouraging a sharing of experience(s). This is achieved by avoiding direct theorizing and instead presenting the ideas as common sense so that the participant can identify with the various scenarios. For example, Whitaker (1993) puts us in touch with 'toxic pedagogy' in which we can begin to understand the formative influences on us and 'the processes by which the potential of children and their actualizing tendency is contained, inhibited and sometimes crushed during the process of upbringing' (p.33). While Ellison (1990a) enables us to see how we can be a victim of culture where there can be a 'conspiracy of silence', which prevents us from admitting to being stressed because it can be seen as a sign of weakness and therefore it hinders the implementation of stress management plans (p.14). Furthermore, Savage (1989) considers communication to be fundamental to effective management and presents the conditions in which rumours are generated and spread to the detriment of organizational and personal health; the way forward is an exhortation to the reader to understand their role within rumour management. Any response to reading such materials and going through the experiential processes is clearly personal, as are the ethical issues of how, during the process, the individual interacts with other colleagues inside the work context.

The general process can be supplemented by a range of specialist products, dealing with particular needs, such as assertiveness (Back et al., 1991; Gillen, 1992), negotiation skills (Lowe and Pollard, 1989; Fisher and Ury, 1991; Ury, 1991), confidence building (Jeffers, 1991), time management (Blanchard et al., 1989; Godefroy and Clark, 1989; Ellison, 1990b) and decision-making (Blanchard and Johnson, 1983; Johnson, 1992). The materials invite the reader to reflect on their context, and think through their experiences and what they mean for their own development as a person and as a professional manager. This has value in enabling the individual to focus on themselves and to recognize the importance of responsibility and choice, and what matters to him or her in life.

Much of what is contained in self-management materials is common sense, but it is packaged in such a way as to stimulate the type of re-evaluation that usually only happens when there is a major life trauma. Time management strategies are useful in enabling us to see a sense of purpose and the importance of performance, rather than seeking comfort in old patterns of working. Self-esteem and assertiveness strategies have the potential to enable effective communication to take place between adults, rather than the poor communication that leads to harassment and hostile working conditions. Furthermore, Jeffers (1991) argues that we are all afraid at different times in our professional and personal lives, but some of us are better at handling it than others. The key is to control the chatterbox in our heads and how we can talk ourselves into negative attitudes and behaviours. Therefore, understanding and using self-management strategies to explore the relationship between the internal and external worlds for the individual, and recognizing how the individual can take control and need not be a victim is of value. The potential for transformation is enormous, and the literature on self-management describes the before and after. Trotter (1993) shows the educational professional as the vulnerable victim of external demands:

> Working in education you face a daily treadmill. Through a succession of days, weeks, terms, academic years, you provide a professional service to learners, colleagues, bosses, parents, employers, authorities, and society. Sometimes it goes well, sometimes you struggle to survive the day. As well as teaching you have to manage learning, resources, people – and yourself. Circumstances don't get easier – there is continual pressure to implement change: new curricula, new forms of exams, new schedules of testing and associated administration, new institutional arrangements. All this in a climate of resource constraints, increasing disruptiveness, even physical attacks on teachers. Yet you keep going, getting some satisfaction when you see your learners develop and succeed. But the process wears you down. What about some time and space for *you* to restore and renew yourself? (p.1)

As a result of going through the process we have the efficient, empowered and gutsy educational professional within the learning organization, and:

> This adds up to everyone exercising a greater degree of *self management*, aligning their efforts with others through allegiance to corporate values and missions, rather than via the external regulation of job descriptions, management by objectives and hierarchical supervision.   (Pedlar *et al.*, 1994, p.4)

However, what is not recognized in the literature is that the processes can create a false empowerment and hence a new vulnerability. The individual teacher is encouraged to seek a stability between the internal and external worlds rather than to use the strength of their internal world to seek a transformation of the external. Therefore we can characterize self-management as firstly, a fear generating industry; and, secondly, a means of ensuring managerialist accountability for performance.

Self-management can be identified as an industry that creates the very insecurities it aims to provide solutions for. Much of what is written and advocated in self-management strategies is not supported by research evidence. It is a quick, short-term fix to a problem that is externally identified and defined, as illustrated by the slimming industry. If not to stretch the analogy too far, just as the failure of crash diets can lead to eating disorders, we have not yet had the research evidence to test out whether self-management strategies do lead to self-empowerment, or to human interaction disorders.

The restructuring of education in the form of self-managing and self-governing educational institutions means that educational professionals have become increasingly accountable, but without the authority to effect real change. Empowerment is meant to be a key aim, with the teacher enabled to meet the needs of the child in the management context where those needs are defined and best responded to: the classroom (at what is often termed the producer–consumer interface). This right to manage in the classroom in order to develop the quality of teaching and learning is supported by a rhetoric of collegiality and consensus-building through teams who participate in policy development and implementation. This is rhetoric rather than reality; the 'empowered teacher' does not have real 'ownership', but rather there is a covert form of control, or what Ozga and Lawn (1988) identify as collegiate 'surveillance':

> Current developments in school management ... involve the establishment of senior management teams who will, collaboratively, be responsible for ensuring that the school is carrying out its agreed and specified policies. Given the pressure on schools to be accountable to clients, and to attract clients through achieving high performance levels, the monitoring and surveillance functions of these teams is bound to be increased. Again, because schools must attract to survive, the pressure on such teams to eradicate 'problems' and establish smooth production is correspondingly greater. Deviations from, or variations on school policy are likely to have less chance of survival. In primary schools, the status of the class teacher is threatened by the quasi-managerial functions of postholders, and the growth of supervisory functions implicit in collegiality. (p.326)

The impact of this managerialist agenda is directly connected to self-management. Within this type of context self-management has a dual purpose: firstly, to put the emphasis on the individual to develop the skills and competences which enable him or her to be inducted into an externally defined agenda; and secondly, to provide a mechanism whereby individuals who find this agenda difficult are able to come to terms with an impossible management context. Self-management is the legitimization of Thatcherism: it enables the individual to cope with the challenge to the organization as a collective process, such as how to negotiate a contract, how to deliver performance indicators, how to win a bigger proportion of the performance related pay deal, and how to be inspected. If the problem in organizations is one of efficiency, effectiveness and economy, then the issue is about individual performance, which must be self-managed if empowerment is to be realized. The individual might go through the process outlined in Table 2.1, and they may be able to solve some perceived problems, but problem-solving is designed 'to make relationships and institutions work smoothly by dealing effectively with particular sources of trouble' (Cox, 1981, p.129). However, individuals live and work in collectives and within unjust social and economic structures that can only be debated by a more critical approach, and therefore the individual needs to ask questions that are missing from Table 2.1 and are illustrated in Table

Table 2.2. Self-management: a wider agenda

- Why is my school/college structured in the way it is?
- How is my school/college changing and what are the implications for myself and my colleagues?
- How can we inform and be a part of the social and political debate about the types of changes taking place?

Table 2.3. Self-management: a critical agenda

- Why has the self-management business grown?
- Why do in-service and Master's programmes contain sessions and modules on self-management.
- Why are books and manuals on self-management being produced, and is there accountability beyond the market?

2.2. Furthermore, the educational professional needs to ask questions about who or what is constructing self-management as a knowledge-base, as illustrated in Table 2.3.

This critical agenda has important implications for teachers and in-service providers in the content, structure and processes involved in professional development. If the educational professional asks these types of questions then they can ask: do I have to manage my time because I really am inefficient and ineffective, or because the tasks I have to perform are impossible within the framework of 1265 hours/professional contracts? In reflecting on my values I can either embrace the niche marketing position of the institution explicit in the vision and mission, or leave. Resistance is policy terrorism rather than policy discourse. This is particularly pertinent to the changing education workforce with restructuring, regrading and the growth of part-time and temporary contracts (Elliott and Hall, 1994). Pluralism is expensive for the individual and the institution. Problem-making rather than problem-solving prevents the right to manage from operating. The concept of the right to manage (i.e. I have a right to manage my time as an individual manager, and the institution has the right to manage the human resource management processes) is an important development and can help to facilitate higher standards in educational institutions. But, what about the right to be dependent? This goes beyond the concept of the self-managing educational institution and raises issues about how the collective, and the state in particular, is conceptualized. The dependency of the parasite is not something to be advocated, but neither should we be promoting the delusion of self-management.

Valuing of the self cannot be an isolated activity and, as White (1987) has argued, the institution has a responsibility to the self-esteem of its members. The danger of self-management processes are that they will transfer whole institutional problems to the individual, and just as the institution's relationship is currently based on managerialist marketing concepts such as the *listening school* so the teacher becomes the *listening practitioner* and must seek solutions to the problems encountered in order to maintain positive accountability both internally and externally. The institution and the professional are dependent on parents, community and society to achieve high standards, and for the quality of teaching and learning. What is missing from education management products is the *vocal school* and the *vocal teacher*, in which professionals can contribute to the political, economic, social and technological debates that affect educational processes. Therefore continuous professional development (CPD) becomes a forum for the facilitation of knowledge, skills and status to engage in policy discourse from the staffroom to county hall to quality journals. Developing research skills is central to this and is where the real partnership between higher education and schools can be made. This is illustrated in Table 2.4.

Table 2.4. The vocal teacher and the vocal school

- Action research to find out and describe what is happening
- Action research to explain what is happening
- Action research to emancipate from what is happening
- Action research to transform and create the future
- Action research to network and collaborate

While research in schools has grown as a management information gathering process, such as data collection for forecasting and costing, and audits on the progress of policy initiatives, there is scope through CPD for a more radical approach. Self-management courses are an ideal opportunity to explore the real social and economic problems faced by practitioners, and to develop the concepts and process of action research (Elliott, 1991; Lomax, 1995) and emancipatory research (Lather, 1986), in which the participant can know, understand and have an impact on what it means to manage the self and others in an unjust world. Kemmis (1991) has shown that this is not naive because emancipatory action research is 'not a thing' but a 'notion' in which

> it does no more than give form to a particular kind of democratic aspiration to engage in changing the world as well as interpreting it. It offers an embryonic, local form of connecting research with social, educational and political action in complex practical circumstances. In this, it is similar to the aspiration sloganised by the environmental movement in the words 'think globally, act locally'. (pp.60–1)

Summary

In using the Jurassic Management metaphor I am at one with Inglis (1985), who has argued that

> what I am trying to represent is a rough-and-ready scheme of mind in which metaphor, as an essential feature of language (a feature without which there could hardly *be* language), meets the imagination, the human faculty by which the vision and re-vision of mere events is turned into experience of an intelligible, meaning-bearing sort. The case is that the structures of our metaphors not only frame our seeing and understanding of the world, but constitute that world; they are its ground and being. (p.26)

The metaphor has highlighted the issue of meaning in the world of education: what is the purpose of education management? What does the Education Management Industry think it is doing in trying to make teachers better managers? Is there more to education management than meets the eye when browsing through catalogues and along bookshop shelves?

Engagement with self-management products brings sharply into focus that a review and debate within the field of education management needs to focus on several issues. Firstly, there is a lack of reflection and reflexivity within the Education Management Industry. This is illustrated by Ozga (1992), who finds that of all the weaknesses identified the

> most striking, and most significant, is the absence of any reflection within these texts on the origins and dimensions of the field of study they seek to expound. The impression that this is an area of teaching, research and publication without a sense of itself, of its intellectual origins and characteristics, is very strong. And this is a very significant absence, as self-consciousness in the subject area might generate self-criticism. (p.279)

The challenge here for the Education Management Industry is whether it can crack open the certainty of the management imperative, and consider whether there are alternative models for school effectiveness.

Secondly, there is a lack of a historical perspective, and this is illustrated in the uncritical acceptance of the self-managing school and the right to manage (Anderson and Dixon, 1993). Codd (1993) has identified the detrimental effects of this acceptance:

> Managerialism produces an organizational culture that is hierarchical, competitive, individualistic and highly task-oriented. It is a culture that is totally alien to the New Zealand experience, and if it is imposed upon schools, it is a culture that tends to be undemocratic and wasteful of human initiative and capacity. (p.159)

Concerns about education management products that have facilitated the adoption of the self-managing school and are disconnected from history have been raised by Ball (1993), who in his critique of Hargreaves and Hopkins's (1991) prescription for *The Empowered School* states:

> The Hargreaves and Hopkins book has only one index entry for 'finance'. This approach is very process-oriented; it is value-free, content-free management (in the sense that good practice is entirely a matter of process). It is the management of anything or nothing (and this is profoundly disturbing). It divorces management practices from values and from politics. The book also has only one index entry for ' values'. It is technically-oriented, rational and apolitical. There are no index entries for 'conflict'. This is management in the best of all possible schools. It is anodyne and reassuring and does a great deal to legitimate management to the professional audience. (p.67)

The challenge here for the Education Management Industry is whether it can see events as being something more than what has created a management imperative.

Thirdly, there is a limited conceptual understanding of the role of theory, and in particular, feminist critiques have shown that management is a masculine world. Adler *et al.* (1993) have shown in particular that they

> found that most of the literature on educational management and on theories of management and organization ignored women, either by making the assumption that all managers are male or by assuming a 'gender-free' position. (p.3)

They go on to cite the work of Shakeshaft (1987), who has provided a critique of research in the field as assuming male and female experiences are the same and therefore generalizations are acceptable. For example, Maslow's (1943) theory of motivation and self-actualization is recognized as being gendered:

> This theory is problematic for women as it indicates to women that self-actualization can be achieved by sex-role fulfilment or denial, while men are led towards devaluing the experience of the home. Maslow applies a value scale to the different needs. He ranks self-actualization, affiliation and self-esteem in descending order, thus matching traditional male values. Maslow presents the self-actualized woman as one who has made it in a man's world.
>
> (Adler *et al.*, 1993, p.7)

Feminist critiques of education management theory and its 'use' of theory developed in other settings, cultures and times raise problems about whether theory can help to describe, evaluate and explain the current professional lives of teachers.

Fourthly, current events and problems are disconnected from the policy context, and critiques have tended to focus on the work of Caldwell and Spinks (1988) and the self-managing school. Demaine (1993) has argued that

> their account is politically coy rather than naive. They acknowledge, briefly, that the policies being pursued by the Conservatives in Britain will lead to self-managing schools and that, 'What is proposed in Britain is potentially the most far-reaching development in any of the countries considered' (p.9); but they have nothing to say about the politics of the New Right, or about the extensive criticism of right-wing education policy in Britain. (p.40)

Walford (1993) adds further to the growing debate about Caldwell and Spinks (1992):

> It is a sad reflection of their depoliticized view of educational administration that, even by 1992, they have not recognized the underlying purpose of the 1988 Education Reform Act in England and Wales. They seem to assume that all government will 'naturally' wish to promote equity, and that it is only administrative difficulties which stand in the way of such ends. But the British government has no interest in equity in educational provision. (p.240)

The consequences of the uncritical acceptance of the self-managing school within education management products have been identified by Ball (1993):

> All too often in policy research and in the texts of self-management, the focus of attention is entirely upon the strengths and weaknesses, faults and difficulties of individual schools. The role of policy-makers within the state in creating dilemmas and contradictions with which schools must deal is ignored. The state is left in the enviable position of having power without responsibility. (p.77)

Therefore an area for reflection for education management participants is to consider whether they are legitimizing New Right policies rather than empowering the teaching profession to engage in a debate about them.

Fifthly, research is based on narrow techniques, and there is very little evidence of ethnography and research as praxis (Lather, 1986). Furthermore, research can be seen as legitimizing the Thatcherite managerial revolution to the detriment of teacher professionalism. As Ball (1990b) has argued about the school effectiveness movement:

> The ideological work done by effectiveness research, linked to notions like accountability, school review, and school improvement, should not be underestimated. The cruder manifestations of the conservative political critique of schools have been reworked into versions of surveillance and monitoring that 'fit' into the preferred teacher discourse of professionalism. In effect, teachers are trapped into taking responsibility for their own 'disciplining' through schemes of self-appraisal, school improvement, and institutional development. Indeed, teachers are urged to believe that their commitment to such processes will make them more professional. (p.162)

These criticisms of education management are themes that run through this book, and they will be explored in succeeding chapters.

CHAPTER 3

Ignorance

This chapter is about the promotion of ignorance by the Education Management Industry. As Inglis (1985) has stated:

> Management indeed turns out to mean persuading others to agree with a more or less good grace on ends which are systemic and unavailable to question. Technique and skills are key words in these trainings, never judgement or reason, nor admiration nor disgust. Indeed the strange ring of this latter coinage takes the measure of its exclusion from the vocabulary of social (and therefore moral and political) arrangements. Such concepts denote, at least in their earlier sense, a moral meaning whose reference could be settled by appeal to an impersonal rationality independent of personal preference. Quite rapidly, the complex but consistent advance of the doctines of the unfettered non-social self (radical personalization, the freeing of the self from all structures), the detachment of the true person from the occupation of social roles, and the making almost synonymous of the expression of personal feelings with the structure of morality – the moral theory known as emotivism – all served to bring about a social order whose principles of cohesion are no longer open to critical reflection and dissent, but are consequently irredeemable, though constantly changing. (p.101)

Such a lengthy quotation has relevance in establishing the theme of this chapter by expertly showing how the separation of the person from the manager has considerable implications for the teacher's capacity to engage in a reflexive learning process. Knowledge creation is aborted. Can the 'truth' be captured through the manufacture and commercial distribution of self-completing proformas and attitude surveys? Do these tools move our knowledge and understanding of schools forward? Having read and reviewed a vast number of education management products, what becomes clear from the proformas, the management cycles and the clairvoyant predictions of what problem the reader is about to face next, is that knowledge is reduced to unproblematic patent medicines.

There is some acknowledgement from within the broader range of education management publications that this is an issue, but the level and type of debate is minimal. For example, Whitaker (1993) notes the following about the Quality Movement:

Total Quality Management (TQM) has arrived on the scene in a flurry of activity and excitement. In a world desperate for solutions to increasing confusion, new bandwagons have a seductive attraction about them ... There is something of a competitive stampede about this latest management novelty as if its mere adoption will bring about success. (p.149)

Wallace and Hall (1994) note the simplicity of much that can be found in education management products:

Practical handbooks for senior staff (e.g. Trethowan, 1985; Nicholson, 1989; Davies *et al.*, 1990; Bell, 1992), often drawing on concepts and techniques developed in organisational settings other than education, are strong on exhortation and practical tips for effective teamwork, and also warn against various pitfalls. As long as the tips are followed faithfully, such handbooks imply that effective teamwork will ensue. There is little acknowledgement of tension between the perception of a management hierarchy and the view that members have an equal contribution to make to team decisions, or of consequences of this tension for SMT effectiveness. (p.14)

Book reviews are often the place where reflection and reflexivity can take place. However, a review of some of the journals primarily dedicated to education management illustrates some important limitations. The *International Journal of Education Management* provides a synopsis of each book and takes a generally celebratory approach, which often reads more as publicity soundbites rather than a review. Within this journal, books are: 'practical', 'thought-provoking', 'invaluable reading', 'essential reading', or 'welcomed'. Within the prestigious BEMAS journal, *Educational Management and Administration*, amidst some very engaging and thought-provoking reviews, there are examples in which there is a general positive view of what products are doing for practising managers rather than what the publication means for the field of education management. The following is a sample:

(1)   Young (Vol.15 (1), 1987), in reviewing three books from the Fontana/Collins *Successful Manager* series, concludes that they provide 'food for thought for the education service' (p.80). Therefore individual reflection on personal goals, time and career etc., is an activity that can be displaced from the policy context.

(2)   Hesse's (Vol. 15 (3), 1987) review of Craig's (1987) *Primary School Management in Action* is direct about the practical focus and use of the book not only in Great Britain, but also in Germany, and in fact says it 'can be recommended to headteachers of schools everywhere as a useful volume' (p.234). Nearly ten years on and in the post-ERA (Education Reform Act 1988) context we need to ask when does a 'useful' practitioner-driven book become a 'useless' and outdated product? When will we know or who will tell us?

(3)   Caswell's (Vol.23 (2), 1995) review of Lawrence and Vachon's (1995) *How to Handle Staff Misconduct – A Step by Step Guide* identifies this as a 'self-programming manual' and focuses mainly on the technical content of relevance, ease of use and transferability from the USA context. The policy context is noted as providing an imperative for such a book to be on a head-teacher's bookshelf:

> LMS school heads still have their personnel advisors in county hall (though for how long?) to manage these affairs. GMS colleagues can use their services also, but at a cost to their schools' beleaguered budgets. (p.142)

However, there is no discussion about whether this is the most professional way in which to lead and manage teachers. And so on!

In other educational journals fundamental questions are being asked. A particular focus of the *Cambridge Journal of Education* shows reflection and promotes issues for debate:

(1)   Downes's (Vol. 21 (1), 1991) review of West and Bollington's (1990) *Teacher Appraisal – a practical guide for schools* is very complementary and asserts that 'every school should have a copy' (p.105), but it is also realistic when relating the so-called 'practical guide' to the under-resourcing in schools and the Government's agenda:

> This is perhaps not the place to comment too extensively on Government priorities, but it seems to me that the creation of an elaborate and expensive apparatus for checking pupils' achievements against externally determined criteria should have been introduced after and not before an appraisal scheme like the one outlined in this book ... The clear way to improve the quality of education in this country is by motivating, encouraging, valuing and re-training teachers; elaborate testing, finance-driven management systems, market-place philosophies may have their place but they come a long way behind the appraisal process so clearly exemplified in this book. (p.105)

(2)   A review of Hargreaves and Hopkins's (1991) *The Empowered School: the management and practice of development planning* by Davies (Vol. 22 (2), 1992) illustrates the concern about the disconnection from the policy context, when he states, 'my experience of schools suggests that we ignore the social and political infrastructure at our cost' (p.264).

(3)   In the same volume MacDonnald (Vol. 22 (2), 1992) reviews Barker's (1991) book, *The Cambridge Management Workshop: professional development and practical guidance for school life in the 90s*, and he questions the value of 'off-the-shelf' materials:

LEEDS METROPOLITAN UNIVERSITY LIBRARY

> It has been my experience ... that taking someone else's ready
> made training materials and using them, however flexibly, is
> usually nowhere near as effective as devising your own. The
> main advantage ... is that it should save time, the other is that
> through research, trialling etc., the materials should be better
> than any you can devise on your own. Even given these points it
> still comes down to effective use, and 'ready-mades' need to be
> particularly good if they are to be used effectively. (p.267)

He goes on to conclude that:

> ... it seems to me that this book does not meet its own stated
> purpose. It is quite evidently a set of published materials used
> originally in a particular context and has not successfully made
> the transition to a set of materials with more universal applica-
> tion ... (p.268)

(4) Fox's (Vol. 22 (1), 1992) review of Aylett's (1991) *Managing a
New Era: an educational management training pack* shows concern
about the lack of an understanding of teaching and learning:

> This pack is a good example of the inadequacy of strategies and
> skills uncritically culled from *industrial* and *commercial* manage-
> ment, to deal with the increasingly critical task of managing the
> complexity and messiness of teaching and learning. (p.119)

Furthermore he is unrelenting in his criticism of 'management
by ringbinder':

> This pack is a belated jumping on a rather dated management
> bandwagon. The contents have little to do with the real educa-
> tional issues affecting school management in the 1990s. At best it
> provides basic low-level training for management, with little to
> do with education. At worst it is an expensive way of buying a
> ring binder. (p.119)

While the bandwagon may be dated, since this review publishers' catalogues have continued to expand with such products.

Comments and observations in book reviews are valuable and could
provide an opportunity for the participants within the Education
Management Industry (assuming they read each other's books and articles)
to stop and think. Reviewers often make reference to the headteacher's
bookshelf and the merits of a particular publication being allowed to be
placed upon it, but the importance of educational leadership is usually in
storage rather than within reaching distance of the busy headteacher.

Two recent books that stand out as having the potential to encourage and
support the Education Management Industry in undertaking a reflective
and reflexive process are Davies (1990) and Bottery (1992). Both are
concerned with the technical and skills approach to management, and what
impact this has for schools operating within a democracy. Davies (1990)

focuses primarily on the dilemmas involved in school goals in relation to equity and efficiency at a time when performance indicators put more emphasis on the latter. The strength of this work is not just the international approach to discussing these issues, but also in showing how 'school organizational problems are presented as *technical* problems, which ignore the power relationships and the structured inequalities around which schools are organized' (p.5). She goes on to show further that:

> The uncritical acceptance of industrial or bureaucratic metaphors within educational institutions means a tying of these institutions to the corporate sector, and provides the means for similar sorts of control mechanisms both of the schools and within the schools. Providing management training only for Heads and senior staff cements a divide between the work of teaching and the work of organizing teaching, in a way that in fact has not traditionally been associated with the enterprise of education in many parts of the world. (pp.5–6)

Bottery's (1992) analysis looks at managerialism at work within schools from the point of view of values. In order to understand the ethics of educational choice Bottery asks the question that is clearly missing from educational management products: what is the purpose of schools and education within a democracy? Such a question enables Bottery (1992) to assert that managerialism is profoundly undemocratic:

> Where teachers and pupils are defined and treated as low in an objectively defined hierarchy, they are less likely to develop managerial understanding and expertise than those who work in a structure which fosters respect for different opinions and judgements and expertise, regardless of their place in a formal hierarchy. Individuals working within a rigid hierarchical structure are also less likely through this experience to believe that their opinion counts for anything, or their actions can affect anything. This is not fertile soil, then, for the development of a truly democratic form of society, in which citizens genuinely and actively participate. (p.3)

Furthermore, the rapid adoption of the free-market philosophy as liberation from bureaucracy elevates self-interest and promotes competition at the expense of democratic values. Therefore management is not value-free and the call for reflection in the field is evident in the well-argued case that there is a 'danger of transferring concepts from other organisations to schools in an insensitive and undiscriminating manner' (p.8). As Bottery (1992) so clearly illustrates, theory is a product of the socio-economic times in which it is developed, and the disinterested view of the educational professional towards theory has made education managers 'prey to invasion from the theories of other, more thoroughly worked, areas' (p.21).

The relationship between education management and business management is one area on which the broader field of education management does debate and reflect (Bottery, 1994). In Harries-Jenkins's (1984) review of the education management literature he asserts that the 'comparative approach conventionally adopts commercial and industrial management as a reference point' (p.216). The debate tends to have a binary focus of *for* or *against* and is concerned with 'borrowing from' or 'transferring from' or 'dipping into' business and commercial models. Hodgkinson (1978) recognizes the importance of organizational settings but argues that:

> There is a freemasonry in the upper echelons of administration, a commonality of problems encountered and strategies adopted which seems to support the assertion that administration is a generalism. (p.7)

However, before the 1988 Education Reform Act those writing from within the field of education tended to argue that 'education institutions are different' (Glatter, 1972) or 'a special case' (Howell, 1978). Al-Khalifa (1986) looks at the work of Mintzberg (1973) in his identification of ten generic roles of the manager, such as leader, mentor, negotiator and entrepreneur, and goes on to argue that:

> It is clear … that, although a manager may perform the ten roles, the role classification does not provide a description of managerial behaviour in a way which is likely to illuminate the essential character of the work … Indeed, most of Mintzberg's roles could equally well be used to describe the work of mother and housewife, but such a description would tell us little about the meaning and skills involved in such work. (p.228)

Al-Khalifa (1986) raises serious questions about the research and motives upon which the case for generalizability is made. Firstly, she sees a connection between Mintzberg's 'management roles' and the training imperative:

> It would appear that Mintzberg was committed to establishing generalizations about management in order to develop standardized training... (p.228)

Secondly, Al-Khalifa raises doubts about comparisons, arguing that like is not compared with like. Lists of management skills can be made and applied to the school. However, 'what is missing from these comparisons is an account of the organizational life of the school and the significance of this for managerial work' (p.231). Furthermore, the field does debate the identification of variables that make educational institutions different. The types of variables identified according to Harries-Jenkins (1984, p. 217) tend to be:

- the activities of educational institutions;
- the uniqueness of educational goals;
- the limited level of professionalism among teachers;
- the loose structure of schools and colleges;
- uncertain output measurement;
- complexity of public control.

What is interesting about the post-1988 period is that there is a general acknowledgement of the growth in influence and utilization of business and industrial models, but the tone of the debate has shifted. Pre-1988, writers like Glatter (1972), Howell (1978), Harries-Jenkins (1984, 1985) and Al-Khalifa (1986) could write with an element of certainty that educational institutions had differences that had to be acknowledged and celebrated. Al-Khalifa (1986) promotes Handy's (1984) assertion that 'Schools would be wise to be different'.

However, this viewpoint is currently somewhat scarce and in the main tends to be accepting of business models in a way that Hatcher (1994) describes as 'largely totemic'. Concerns about 'subservience to non-educational values' (Downie, 1990, p.158) have been glossed over, with the current emphasis being on how we manage the connection. The imperative for education management is conceptualized as being about the transfer processes especially in management training. This issue is not new and was identified by Glatter in 1972:

> If the cleavage between theory and reality in management training is ever to be repaired it must be by *the use of teaching and learning methods which reveal the applicability of the material presented.* (author's own emphasis) (p.8)

More recently Bottery (1992) has produced an excellent review of how far we have come since Glatter raised this issue of applicability. He shows *how* business management has been used and debates *what* can be borrowed. He goes on to argue that

> there would seem to be a number of things that could profitably be translated from other contexts and used in education, but they are not the kind of things which can be taken down ready-made from the shelf and bolted onto the educational organization. They must be moulded, adapted, re-invented almost. In so doing, one is refusing the quick prescription from those who should know better, and one is urging sensitive adaptation by practitioners. Correct utilisation, then, necessarily demands the acceptance of teacher professionalism.' (pp.127–8)

This seems a very sensible approach and one that practitioners in their engagement with education management products would find difficult to argue with. However, the 'acceptance of teacher professionalism' is essential to the debate, but as I have illustrated so far the managerial agenda negates the right to resist and to question the management imperative. Furthermore, it isn't enough to turn the issue around and argue that business can learn from education (McIllhatton *et al.*, 1993). I would like to see education management stop asking: '*Is* a school different or similar to a factory or a shop?' and instead ask: '*Why* is that comparison being made?' Are we concerned with transferring the digested outcomes of the application of certain aspects of the social sciences to business management, or should we return to the full array of social science disciplines that Baron and Taylor (1969) had such high hopes for in the late 1960s? Baron and Taylor (1969) argued that

> educational administration has just as much to gain from close affiliations with social philosophy, sociology, social psychology and economics. Even the most practical issues, such as those concerned with the siting and building of schools, the appointment of teachers and the subjects a child should study depend upon

the interpretation at some point in the sequence of decision-making of basic concepts of equality, freedom and justice. (p.8)

This now seems like a different world and in the 1980s King (1984) made a case for the sociology of organizations to be given recognition because it 'is concerned with the search for understanding and explanation, that is, theories to explain the "what happens" of organisations, in contrast to the prescriptive "what ought to happen" of organisation theory' (p.59). Furthermore, this approach would facilitate *education* in which there are 'learning processes implying an understanding that transcends particular experiences or circumstances', rather than *training*, which 'implies the preparation for fairly specific tasks where there are established criteria for performance' (p.60). King (1984) goes on to identify that the wide adoption of training from initial teacher training (ITT) through to headteachers is significant and:

> may be in the desire of these authorities to promote greater standardisation of educational processes, based upon prescriptions of 'good' practice, in pursuit of greater 'efficiency' in conditions of financial stringency. This would mean an erosion of current professional autonomy. (p.60)

However, King's (1984) case for the importance of sociology seems to have been lost and contrasts dramatically with other writers within the field. Watson (1982) has argued that the role of the academic is not to provide the practitioner with 'tips' or 'theory' but to assist the practitioner in developing:

- diagnostic skills in identifying the most significant elements within the situation which confront him;
- an understanding of a range of possible strategies;
- an ability to match strategies to the salient elements of a situation so that 'closer match' choices can be made;
- the skills of operational planning and implementation (including monitoring and control). (Watson, 1982, p.17)

Management is therefore something more than intuition and the irrational application of experience, and it should not be hindered by descriptive and explanatory theories. Rather, applied management is about the skills and competences for improving performance and 'the development of capability' (Glatter, 1979, p.32). The case is being made for teachers as managers to be reflective practitioners, but as we have already seen self-management and other products are able to develop this type of capability at the expense of professional capability. In the struggle to establish respectability as a field of applied and relevant practice, the Education Management Industry has failed to recognize the nature of the practitioners on whose behalf it was claiming to work.

If the Education Management Industry does not facilitate the practitioner's engagement with theory from the broad range of social sciences, then professional capability to think, read, question, understand, argue and feel passion is undermined. For example, students of education management are normally given access to the Hawthorne studies (Pugh, 1990) and the learning outcomes for managers, such as the importance of group relationships and supervision in relation to worker output. Therefore good practice for the manager in using diagnostic skills and identifying possible strategies is to recognize the importance of the information networking within the organization. However, unless the sociology of organizational behaviour is investigated then what is defined as a skill or a non-skill goes unquestioned, and furthermore, what is often missing is a key learning outcome from the Hawthorne studies – the importance of 'organizational processes related to sex based power differentials' (Acker and Van Houten, 1992, p.22). Managers need to be in touch with the actual research processes that generate particular management skills, otherwise schools will be importing ways of working that have already led to discrimination among women and ethnic groups. Within education management products women are either ignored or there is an 'and women' approach with a section or chapter added in. The issue of gender and its central role in structuring organizational behaviour and relationships has yet to inform educational management products.

Reflection, reflexivity and revisionism requires a catholic and eclectic review of the field by education management participants. This is not easy, as the certain world of the ringbinders would be challenged by doubt and questions. The movement from the academic as a reflective practitioner who is generating education management products to the academic as reflective professional who is contributing to the debate about policy and practice requires what Bottery (1992) calls 'educating dissent' (p.53) rather than education for conformity. He illustrates this by arguing that within schools a pupil's conformity to rules happens through threats of punishment rather than through ownership. It could be argued that the reflective practitioner within the Education Management Industry fears reprisals and therefore conforms to the rules of the marketplace. If the higher education lecturer does not provide problem-solving solutions and eschew theory, then business is lost and income generation targets are not met.

Educating dissent within the Education Management Industry would mean that the field would begin to look very different. Very rarely do you see education management writers expressing doubt and putting forward the view that their ideas are developing and open to the charge of contradiction. For example, White and Crump (1993) celebrate the speculative and exploratory approach of Stephen Ball (1994) when, in his reply to Hatcher and Troyna's (1994) critical discussion of Education Policy Sociology, he states:

But what do I accept from these criticisms? I am certainly ready to confess to contradiction. I continue to hold and want to juggle with and attempt to integrate a set of disparate epistemological and theoretical positions. I see this as productive but not without its problems. In this sense I am no purist. I am interested in an 'applied sociology' which engages with 'real world' issues. I also regard my analytical work as continuing. I see many things needing still to be done. I regard my sociology as an evolving practice and I see sociology in general as having achieved limited effectivity in the analysis of high modern social life. I am not ready for closure or certainty. In a social world where political, national, scientific and medical uncertainties seem to be defining characteristics an absolute sociology seems anomalous, to say the least. (pp.171–2)

The range and type of debate required to produce such reflection and reflexivity is not happening in relation to the growth and development of the Education Management Industry.

Jurassic management theory

An area for reflection within the Education Management Industry is to consider what types of knowledge, skills and understanding do management practitioners need and want? This has to go far deeper than a current fad or bandwagon that is rolling through the publishers' catalogues, but does require consideration of the whole purpose and role of theory for those interested in education and schools in particular.

Hoyle (1986) distinguishes between theory for practice and theory for understanding, and while he recognizes the simplistic nature of the distinction he does characterize management theory as directly linked to practice:

Management theory, as practical theory, is concerned with enabling the practitioner to improve the effectiveness of organizations and, simultaneously, the work satisfaction of members. Thus its focus is on organizational design, leadership, decision-making, communication, etc. (p.15)

Therefore what is useful is what can enable the practitioner to move forward, and in fact we must ensure that theories to enable understanding do not hinder effective management:

these theoretical advances, in their emphasis on phenomenology, micro-politics, symbols, and competing rationalities, though yielding improved ways of understanding organizations, provide little help in the practicalities of running a school and indeed could inhibit the headteacher's capacity to *act*. (p.23)

Furthermore, for Hoyle (1986), it is also the case that relevance and quality are defined by the the person or institution who pays the invoice:

Greenfield (1980) writes that the function of management training is to give the educational administrator a transcendental view of the world and his place within it – true perhaps, but hardly a course objective likely to appeal to funding agencies. (p.23)

There is clear evidence from the vast array of education management products that there is a market or demand for training in specific skills and expert knowledge in, for example, the design and use of management information systems in decision-making, and costing curriculum innovation in order to make a bid to an outside agency. There is also recognition in education management products that this is what managers need, and prefaces, introductions and fly covers are full of statements about how in the post-Education Reform Act (ERA) school there is a management imperative. As a consequence education management has flourished with the *Times Educational Supplement* full of courses, and publishers' catalogues full of books and ringbinders promoting management models and techniques. The trend in the 'tips for managers' can be of value in the way that problem pages can give advice to people in need, but the dominance of this approach is questioning the value of theory, and there is some evidence from education management of a realization of this.

> Management theories can be so mechanistic as to be almost wholly detached from the realities of organizational life. One still encounters management theories which are splendidly rational blueprints for an unreal world. (Hoyle, 1986, p.15)

Even so, such blueprints fill bookshop shelves and my notes from reading these products have a desperate question hidden in the middle: why do I see the same material recycled and used over and over again? Furthermore, rational models and tools are used to manage time (Knight, 1989), teams (Bell, 1992), and budgets (Blanchard *et al.*, 1989).

There is no debate within these types of product about whether rational models are a deficit view of school management, and whether the presentation of a 'systematic' approach could be a recipe for deadening schools. Furthermore, the capability and skill factor for the practitioner in knowing and understanding the how, what and why of utilizing such a handbook is left to the additional purchase of consultancy or a training course. Product developers have tended to deal with this issue by the promotion of key names as 'trusted experts': if you see the name on the cover or the flyer then it is worth the risk of spending £14.99. Others ensure that the book is tied in with a course, or by making their values explicit at the beginning of their handbook. Consider the following:

On school development planning:

> Despite these problems, it is our view that a proactive planning approach is appropriate to the dynamic environment in which schools find themselves, and their need to be responsive to pupils and to changing circumstances.
>
> (Davies and Ellison, 1992, p.3)

On appraisal:

> The concept of appraisal embodied in this document is given below:
>
> > Appraisal of performance is an activity which is central to the effective management of the teaching/learning environment. We see appraisal

as a right of all teachers, something which is done with people rather than to them. It is therefore important that both appraisee and appraiser are actively involved in the process. Rather than adding to the already considerable pressures faced by teachers, appraisal of performance aims to channel the energies of staff towards the essential rather than the superficial.

(Mathias and Jones, 1989, Introduction)

On inspection:

> This book is intended as a practical resource. It examines each stage of the inspection process in the context of what schools can do *proactively* to prepare for inspection. *We believe that the healthiest approach to inspection is one where school leaders inculcate in staff an expectation that they will be confidently operating at the highest level of quality assurances, rather than reacting to externally imposed quality control resulting from inspection.* Periodic inspection then becomes an event which may offer additional insight into the school but does not dominate its planning. Standards and quality will improve *because people want improvement* and not because they are being measured every four years.
>
> (Ormston and Shaw, 1994, p.viii)

Therefore, if the producer–consumer values coincide, you can be comfortable with the problem-solving package contained within the covers. The only difficulty for the consumer is that the vast array of these products means that there is a need for a *Which Report* on consumer testing. The serious point is that these handbooks are based on a narrow view of the practitioner as an educational worker who needs to turn to skills, knowledge and understanding outside of pedagogy and curriculum innovation in order to manage. Much of the education management products suggest that the functions of a school have shifted from the direct teaching of children.

This is a narrow view of knowledge as being purely application-based. This has implications for knowledge generation as well as dissemination. If I write a book for the practitioner on, for example, how to run the school budget, then the knowledge utilized to produce this cannot show the theoretical basis, otherwise I would have to engage the reader in ontology, epistemology and philosophical questions about the theoretical basis on which the claims for practical validity are based. Therefore, writing in the mode of 'management by ringbinder' means that the reader should not be presented with the debate about systems theory but just needs to be shown and convinced by exhortation that it will be useful. A headteacher working in a turbulent environment and facing an OFSTED inspection is conceptualized as making *Kaisen* (continuous improvement) decisions and therefore needs *Kaisen* solutions. This has a huge impact on knowledge production, as the emphasis is more on the packaging than on the substance.

Here we need to consider what Hoyle (1986) calls theory for understanding and there is a clear body of literature in the field of education management which draws on, for example, organization theory, and from this aims to facilitate understanding. In these types of writing, theory is used to describe management contexts, and is often evaluative. Furthermore, there is often a strong normative element in identifying what ought to be the way forward. Again the justification here is that events make it an imperative, but there is a recognition that life is more complex than the 'survival guides'. Bush (1989, 1995) has done a lot of work in developing the status of theory for the practitioner manager and we need to acknowledge that the broader field of education management does engage in debate about the role of theory, whether educational institutions are different and whether managers should be trained or educated. The work of Bush has been important in making theory accessible to practitioners and in giving practical evidence of how it can help effective management. It is to the discredit of the Education Management Industry that it often cannot even acknowledge the importance of this work within its own field. In the immediate post-ERA period, Bush (1989) showed that 'there is no universally applicable explanation, or panacea, for the managerial problems of schools' (p.3) and therefore there is a need to use a range of theories to provide explanatory perspectives. In a case study Bush (1989) applies theory from bureaucratic/structural models, political bargaining and interest group models, and subjective phenomeno-logical models to school structures. He shows how theory can help to understand a particular management problem of the pastoral–academic divide within a high school and identify a way forward through restructur-ing. Subjective theory based on Greenfield (1973) is used to give a longer term perspective, that is, the headteacher changed the structure because it is easier to do that than to change perceptions, but it is the latter that will affect the outcome of the restructuring as a solution.

Bush has gone on to develop his ideas (1995) and he is not alone in debat-ing the role of organization theory. The key issue that dominates the minds of writers is the division between various models and whether this is helpful or not for both the researcher and the practitioner. Lane (1995) argues that there are two competing paradigms: one based on positivism rooted in the assumption that reality is external to the individual, and one based on a 'cultural perspective' in which reality is intrinsic. What concerns Lane is that these paradigms have been generated and are defended by their proponents on the basis of 'truth', and hence are defined and defended as opposites. Lane identifies that he is not the only one to be disillusioned with this approach, and in fact Bush (1995) presents a typology of models in which he raises similar concerns. Bush identifies six models for describing and evaluating educational management in educational institutions: formal, collegial, political, subjective, ambiguity and cultural. What distinguishes the models are the different perspectives on: goals, organizational struc-ture, the external environment and leadership. Bush (1995) does not conceptualize the models as rivals but does identify that:

> The six models discussed in this book represent different ways of looking at educational institutions. They are analogous to windows, offering a view of life in schools or colleges. Each screen offers valuable insights into the nature of

management in education but none provides a complete picture. The six approaches are all valid analyses but their relevance varies according to the context. Each event, situation or problem may be best understood by using one or more of these models but no organization can be explained by using only one approach. In certain circumstances a particular model may appear to be applicable while another theory may seem more appropriate in a different setting. There is no single perspective capable of presenting a total framework for our understanding of educational institutions … (p.143)

This enables an understanding of educational management as being rich and diverse and hence capable of developing a better description and evaluation of the management context. However, the desire to develop a more unified approach is strong, and Bush (1995, pp.150–3) reports on the work of Davies and Morgan (1983), who integrate political, collegial, formal and ambiguity perspectives into a systemic framework in which institutional policy formulation goes through four phases:

- initiation: ambiguity models;
- problem-solving: political models;
- communication and commitment building: collegial models;
- implementation: formal models.

Bush (1995) quite rightly gives recognition to critiques of this in the failure of the framework to acknowledge the importance of subjective models; and furthermore, while the sequential linking of the four models is of value it does not allow for the relevance of context. Bush (1995, pp.148–50) argues quite strongly that there are five 'over-lapping considerations' when trying to understand the validity of the six models:

- size of the institution;
- organizational structure;
- time available for management;
- availability of resources;
- external environment.

Bush (1995) goes on to explore the attempts to synthesize different models into a comprehensive framework, and he argues for a contingency approach. Therefore, rather than there being a rigid structure imposed on managers whereby they go through a sequence of processes, as outlined by Davies and Morgan (1983), the focus is on the manager and the development of 'conceptual pluralism', in which

leaders should choose the theory most appropriate for the organization and for the particular situation under consideration. Appreciation of the various approaches is the starting point for effective action. It provides a 'conceptual tool kit' for the manager to deploy as appropriate in addressing problems and developing strategy. (p.154)

Lane (1995) would agree that these models are therefore basically 'multiple truths' (Lane, 1995, p.63; Bush, 1995, p.154) and goes on to explore how theory interacts with the practitioner in more depth. Bush (1995) leaves the debate by putting the emphasis on the manager and hence the development of contextual competences through management education and training. Lane finds the need to explore what this means for the theorist. If the role of theory is external to the manager in the sense of Davies and Morgan's (1983) synthesis of the four models, then the role of theorists is very limited and doomed to the critique of irrelevance. However, if theory is a product to be consumed as a package or in parts, according to the choice of the manager, then this questions the validity of the theorist. As Lane (1995) states,

> The purpose of the theorist in the field of educational administration is to find ways to represent the behaviour in an educational institution which will provide useful guidance for others in that context. Whatever are these ways, they will be constructs of some kind, whether theories, models or something else. If a theorist cannot do this he or she has nothing to say. But useful guidance means that the theorist's constructs must work for others and, for this to happen, these others are required to judge whether what the theorist says works. (p.74)

In the search to enable the theorists with competing paradigms to move beyond promoting their theoretical stances to effectively describing and evaluating management contexts in order to support practitioners, then he argues that what both the positivist approach (Bush (1995) would argue formal and collegial models) and the cultural approach (Bush (1995) would argue the subjective, political, ambiguity and cultural models) have in common is that they both agree that 'the intentions of actors are too variable for there to be an adequate account of them' (p.68). That is, the positivists would argue that 'it is not necessary to account for intentions since an adequate acceptability of any explanation can be given without them', while the culturalists would argue 'that the acceptability of any explanation rests on the match with intentions and, since these are not accountable, then adequacy lies wholly with (unknowable) intentions' (p.68). If this is the case then there is no way forward: the manager will operate in a contingency framework, while the theorists battle it out in irrelevant seminars and journal articles. Lane (1995) makes the case that the differences between the two approaches are limited and based on false assumptions. Firstly, the positivist and culturalist paradigms are not really theoretical in the sense of being a set of rules, but are just different ways of thinking about the world, and therefore paradigms are invented mental constructs; and, secondly, the apparent agreement by the two perspectives that the intentions of the individual are too many and too varied to be able to be theorized external to the individual is a false assumption. Lane (1995) argues that intentions are structured in the form of choices, and the meaning underpinning this is linked to ethical questions about power and control. Therefore:

The culturalist is right in saying that *all* theory is invented social reality, but wrong to say that intentions cannot be captured in a statement external to an actor. The positivist is right in saying that we can represent social action in a statement which is external to the actor, but wrong to say that that statement excludes any account of intentions. In other words, provided that there exists this agreement on the many and varied intentions (even though the assumption is false), and provided that intentions are structured (which is what the theory of personal constructs suggests), then we have cleared the way to a social construction of behaviour which focuses on intentions. It is this single possibility which may remove the differences between theorists (and perspectives). (p.74)

Lane's (1995) postscript is to acknowledge that the ability of theorists and practitioners to agree or to agree to disagree is unlikely, and 'nor ... is it certain whether a theory of educational administration can be found' (p.76). The uncertainties surrounding the debate about theory within education management are clearly being articulated within the field but seem to be absent from the products which proclaim to be a part of the field.

The Education Management Industry's limited engagement with theory is because it has to present management as more than common sense so that it can take itself and be taken seriously. It is almost as if the debate within the broader field about theory (see *Educational Management and Administration* Vol. 21(3), 1993) doesn't happen because product development and manufacture carries on regardless. It would be useful for the Education Management Industry to engage in exploring whether organization theory does have the ability to explain rather than just describe and evaluate the impact of change on schools. In reading Bush's (1995) work we might be left asking:

(1) Why are schools structured in the way they are? How does it link with the broader structures of the social and economic systems within which schools are located?

(2) How are political models useful in understanding the broader context within which teachers work, e.g. the role of trade unionism and professional associations?

(3) How is the use of subjective models of value in understanding teacher perceptions of how external reforms are having an impact on their working lives?

To investigate these types of questions we need to go into theoretical territory where currently education management products do not go! Locke (1986), editor of *Educational Management and Administration*, presented an editorial called 'Knowing better', in which he drew attention to the combination of practice, theory, policy and history within that particular issue. The question that he raised – 'what kind of knowledge makes a difference to our working lives?' (p.165) – seems to have been distorted by the growth of DIY ringbinders that have flooded the market in the last ten years. There is a different kind of understanding, skills, and knowledge, which education management practitioners are now being denied access to: theory for understanding and *explanation*. It is not denied that practitioners need practical skills and knowledge, but in researching into this and theorizing about it then we might ask: why do they need *particular* types of skill and knowledge? What is the *purpose* of these skills and of knowing particular things? Who is *defining* these skills and knowledge and why? What is the *effect* of this type of knowledge or a particular skill on a teacher's professional status? What is the *impact* on pedagogy and the curriculum? In asking these types of questions the practitioner has to look beyond the narrowness of today's problem and how to solve it, and move beyond it to consider the broader social and economic context in which he or she operates. A lot of education management products help to facilitate this by enabling the practitioner to understand and interact with the environment. However, understanding is narrowly focused around boundary management and there is an acceptance of the consumer model. What education management products do not do is to move into broader questions about *why* we are accepting managerialist concepts such as accountability rather than educational professional concepts such as collegiality. Much deeper questions, such as the purpose and role of education asked by Bottery (1992), are never asked. Why? Hoyle (1986) puts his finger on the button when he states:

> the understandings yielded by organization theory could easily bemuse and confuse the practitioner who tries to struggle with philosophical disputes within fields marked by an arcane scholasticism. (p.15)

In other words, the type of knowledge generated as a result of asking questions about the purposes of education is knowledge for the sake of knowledge and therefore of little use to the practitioner. Hoyle (1986) goes on to show that if we look at issues about power, the state and elites in the way that Marxist and Neo-Marxist writers do then we can explain what is happening and why it is happening, but this has consequences for education management:

> There is a view, particularly a Marxist view, that schools are best understood not through the ideologies which these processes sustain. This view holds that the focus should be on what functions the school performs in relation to society, particularly its relationship with the means of production and the sustaining hegemony. (p.17)

It could be argued that what education management is doing is sustaining and promoting the managerialist hegemony. This allows us to see 'the right to manage' and 'schools make a difference' movements in a different way. Wragg in his Foreword to the *Education Matters* series (in Blanchard *et al.*, 1989) states:

> Each book gives an account of the relevant legislation and background, but, more importantly, stresses the practical implications of change with specific examples of what is being or can be done to make reforms work effectively.

If we accept this, then every education issue becomes a management problem which the school *de facto* has to solve. However, schools cannot manage away all the social and economic injustices which act as barriers to a child's learning. Does education management allow the practitioner to make choices about which problems it can and cannot solve? For Osborne (1990) the answer to the question is clearly no.

> For some, this appears as a rapid move away from the consensus approach to change which characterised education up to the 1970s, and as a move towards imposed solutions at all levels of the service. We should make no mistake about the political nature of these developments, but a horrified throwing in of the towel is no response on the part of those who would manage the service in the interests of pupils. Major management questions start to emerge – questions can only be answered from an *educational management* perspective. (p.3)

Therefore education management products are about prioritizing problem-solving and not about choosing to problem-solve. Osborne (1990) would no doubt see this as defeatist. However, on the other hand it can be seen to be realistic. Real empowerment comes not just from having management knowledge, skills and capability, but also from knowing why you have those competences, why you are using them, what impact it is having on your life as a teacher and as a professional, and why government policy is promoting those competences as being essential prerequisites for leadership.What is evident is that the only solution put forward is a management one and in that sense a whole new education product base and market for higher education.

Jurassic management development

An interesting way of exploring these issues is to consider the management of appraisal. A review of the literature on appraisal shows that it can be seen as falling into one of two types:

- appraisal as an education management technical process;
- appraisal as policy and practice.

The technical processes involved in appraisal are rooted in the external requirement on schools that appraisal must be introduced and managed. Therefore the question to be asked is: how can this process be implemented to further the quality of teaching and learning? The literature promotes the importance of understanding the purpose and hence value system on which the appraisal system adopted is based: developmental or performance review and control. There are handbooks and manuals with proformas; advice; checklists; prepared overhead transparencies for in-service days to support a range of themes, such as self-appraisal, different ways of under-taking classroom observation and how to set SMART (specific, measured, achievable, relevant, timed) targets. This is underpinned by assumptions linked to (but not often openly acknowledged) theory from psychology, change management and systems theory. Such theory is used to solve practical problems, for example, if there is potential resistance to an externally imposed change, how do we convince teachers that it is in their own best interests to make appraisal work? Fullan (1991) can be brought in here to enable teachers to understand that change requires them to be challenged and supported, and furthermore the 'phenomenology' of change enables the LEA, in-service provider and school manager to understand that teacher perceptions make this complex. However, as Anderson and Dixon (1993) have argued,

> while interactionist (e.g. cultural, micropolitical, symbolic) analyses of school life characteristic of the subjectivist paradigm have become more central to the field, they have too often been appropriated by the control-oriented, managerial bias of the objective paradigm. Administrators are encouraged to *manage* the culture of the school, *manage* conflict and *manage* the discourse (i.e. meaning) of the school. (p.54)

Once appraisal is underway, the technical process of how well it is going can be explored through gaining an understanding of outcomes and teacher perceptions of both the technical aspects of the appraisal tasks and events, and their perceptions on its impact on teacher development (Barber *et al.*, 1995; Kyriacou, 1995). Furthermore, once the techniques of appraisal are understood and teachers are convinced of the need for ongoing training in areas such as counselling skills and observation skills, then the debate can rise to a higher level about how appraisal can fit in with whole institutional development. I have argued elsewhere (Gunter, 1996) how the concept of the learning organization borrowed from private sector organizations can be utilized to show the gap between the actual and potential in the link between appraisal and both individual and institutional development. Such eclectic consumerism in relation to 'shopping' for theory is to be valued, and education management could tap into everything that the social sciences has to offer. However, current shopping habits are limited and are linked to rather crude needs analysis and therefore the richness within the social sciences is not in evidence in education management products.

Consider the following:

> I can see that appraisal could be useful, I just think it's a pity it has to be such a formal legalistic thing ... I can see why they want accountability, although I think its definitely a modern fad as well ... it's a growing way of making work for people higher up in the system ...

This is a teacher talking about appraisal. How do we manage this? The handbook approach would provide the teacher/trainer/manager with strategies to enable him or her to understand that their role has changed and therefore be generally comfortable with an externally installed appraisal system. A broader review of the social sciences would enable the teacher/trainer/manager to see the above response in a different way. The teacher might be seen as being rather perceptive in seeing appraisal as an example of the role of the state 'steering at a distance' (Kickert (1991) quoted by Ball (1993, p.65)); or alternatively for those social scientists interested in teachers' work then it might provide evidence of a teacher unwilling to collude with deskilling policies (Anderson and Dixon, 1993).

If we dip into sociology and the work of Foucault (1972) then the teacher's response to appraisal can be understood and explained in a different way. Ball (1990b) has used Foucault's concept of 'moral technology' to understand and explain the impact of appraisal on teachers' professional and personal lives:

(1)   If we try to make appraisal (and other management processes) more efficient, then are we not accepting efficiency as a neutral process, and Ball (1990b) asks 'efficiency for whom' (p.154)?

(2)   If we subject teaching to industrial management processes then the 'curriculum becomes a delivery system and teachers become its technicians or operatives' (Ball, 1990b, p.154), and hence is appraisal a form of control that undermines the professional control of the education processes by teachers?

(3)   If we subject teachers to management control through appraisal then are we not redefining teachers' work in a way that enables it to be 'calculable, describable, and comparable' (Ball, 1990b, p.159)?

Foucault's theoretical concepts enable Ball (1990b) to show appraisal as being a form of 'examination' in which power is exercised even in a process that claims to have the potential to develop teacher ownership and be developmental:

> The appraisal interview has elements both of the confessional and the psycho-analytical encounter, both of which rely upon the dynamics of self-revelation. The appraisees are encouraged to display their shortcomings, to seek out or identify appropriate therapeutic procedures, and to judge themselves and award their own punishment.   (Ball, 1990b, p.161)

Furthermore, Ball (1990b) takes the discussion to a different level of analysis and asks questions about those who are involved in the 'discourses of management and research fields like school effectiveness' (p.165). He argues that this is 'professional job creation' (p.165) in which consultants and trained managers have access to certain types of knowledge that is used to devise procedures which conceptualize the teacher as a subordinate,

> Management is a professional, professionalizing discourse which allows its speakers and its incumbents to lay exclusive claims to certain sorts of expertise – organizational leadership and decision-making – and to a set of procedures that casts others, subordinates, as objects of that discourse and the recipients of those procedures, whether they wish to be or not. (pp.156–7)

This is not a conspiracy by some teachers against other teachers, or by providers of management knowledge against the consumers of that knowledge, but rather an understanding 'of the overall effect of the concatenation of initiatives, constraints, changes in control and decision making, and changes in conditions of work that are having their impact on teachers' daily lives' (Ball, 1990b, p.154).

If appraisal is conceptualized as a technical process then it will enable a manager to implement a policy quickly, with the key stages laid out and the paperwork proformas ready to duplicate and fill in. There is also the potential for continuous improvement as the integration of appraisal into other whole institutional frameworks will allow the proactive manager to see how appraisal could be taken a stage further to solve larger longer-term problems. By engaging people in a therapeutic appraisal interview integrated with consensus team-building, then resistance and sabotage can be managed.

However, if you conceptualize appraisal as policy and practice then it will not be so easy to solve your problems. By exploring social science explanations of policy, for example, the role of the state or the existence of policy elites, or Neo-Marxist arguments about the proletarianization of teachers, then the school manager is in a dilemma. Trade unionism, which had a purpose in highlighting these issues, has been characterized as being 'useless' because it was seen as a barrier, and resistance is characterized as negative. Trade unionism has been replaced by human resource management and therefore we are all individually and collectively responsible (and therefore, the argument goes, are empowered) for the success of the organization. Therefore you cannot resist appraisal or any other managerial tool without being seen to undermine accountability networks, and ultimately job security. Education management as a field of application cannot engage in this type of debate without raising questions about its own raison d'être as competency provision for problem-solving. However, purely focusing on application is sterile and misleading to the practitioner.

The use of Foucault (1972) and his conceptualization of knowledge production and discourse is not found in mainstream education management writing. Even those brave writers who are beginning to acknowledge concerns about 'management-by-ringbinder' products are unable as yet to engage in this type of debate because we are potentially all a part of the moral technology that Ball (1990b) identifies. We are trapped in market structures that promote managerial knowledge and solutions, and Anderson and Dixon (1993) acknowledge this as an issue in the USA:

> Although scepticism regarding site-based management runs high among school practitioners, mandates continue to come from policymakers and administrators, encouraged by educational literature and a new generation of high-priced consultants that promote site-based management without any effort to place it in a larger social or political context. (p.50)

Reflection and reflexivity is therefore very difficult within an education system that has been transformed into a marketplace. Valufacturing (de Bono, 1993) within higher education providers or by individual consultants has not prevented the development of training programmes rooted in moral technology. In spite of concerns in the broad educational literature about competency-based training it is still a growth area from initial teacher training to newly qualified teacher profiles, through to aspiring and in-post headteachers. The recently introduced Headlamp scheme will intensify the trend in which

> leading educational administrators are increasingly chosen on the basis of value-free, managerialist competences rather than distinctive educational understandings and experiences. (Ryan, 1993, p.196)

Kirkham (1995) has argued that an entitlement to a mentor is essential if Headlamp is to be more than 'technical prowess'. Headlamp is complementary to education management products as they both promote what Crichton (1991) calls 'thintelligence' in which:

> They think narrowly and they call it 'being focused'. They don't see the surround. They don't see the consequences. That's how you get an island like this. From thintelligent thinking. Because you cannot make an animal and not expect it to act *alive*. To be unpredictable. To escape. But they don't see that. (p.284)

New teachers and headteachers are being created by the competency movement and it is up to those of us who are still 'alive' to sabotage it.

CHAPTER 4

Busy but blind

Consider the following two quotations:

Quotation 1

'Equally pressing problems have followed the emergence of large scale institutions, both schools and colleges, with complexities of internal organisation and outside relationships of an order different from anything known before. The communications problems of comprehensive schools and technical colleges, the variety of links that they must establish with industry and other educational institutions, and their need to explain their purposes to the wider public all underline the scope of the challenges they have to face.'

Quotation 2

'Schools in the UK are currently faced with a reform package which includes not only a new national curriculum but also changes in school governance, management and funding, changes in the roles of local authorities, in student testing and school inspection, and in pedagogy and classroom organization and changes in teacher training, and teachers' conditions of work and employment. It is easier to capture the scope of change involved by listing those things that remain the same ...'

Both quotations encapsulate the educational context of turbulent and far-reaching changes taking place, and there is much that the writer of quotation 2 would recognize in quotation 1, such as responsiveness to the environment. However, what is different is that quotation 1 gives a broad-brush picture of the macro restructuring that took place in the 1960s and 1970s with comprehensivization, and what quotation 2 gives recognition to is not just the macro but the micro, i.e. the detailed changes to the educational tasks that schools and colleges perform. There is a gap of twenty-four years between the two quotations (quotation 1: Baron and Taylor, 1969, p.4; quotation 2: Ball, 1993, p.63), and during that time practitioners have looked for help and support in the implementation of policy initiatives. Poster (1976) notes that the Burnham Report 1956 'provided the opportunity for the introduction into the structure (in a school) of middle management', but he also argues that changes in schools were taking place 'in the absence of any significant thinking or writing about education management' (p.20). What is evident is that in the twenty years since Poster's book on school decision-making, the Education Management Industry has not procrastinated in creating and responding to the perceived needs of practitioners. While there has been much activity on the part of the Education Management Industry during that time, we need to consider how history and events have been treated within education management products.

A cursory glance at education management products shows agreement with Osborne's (1990) view that:

> we should be looking not at such practice in the past but rather in the future. (p.2)

There is a strong emphasis on the here and now within education management products so that the strategies advocated are seen as valid to the practitioner in order to solve the problem(s) and move the organization forward. Events are often narrated as a means of establishing a management imperative, i.e. the management model provides the solutions (and of course job creation for the industry). Consider the following extract:

> Nonetheless, the White Paper 'Choice and Diversity' places upon schools and colleges – and also the residual parts of Education Departments – the requirement to articulate a 'clear academic mission'. This book shows how the necessary information collection, analyses and management processes can be undertaken in simple, yet rigorous, ways so as to produce an appropriate PLAN which will guide, inform and motivate the school and its 'partners'.
> (Puffitt *et al.*, 1992, pp.vii–viii)

Therefore planning, and more specifically business planning for schools, is legitimized as a professional activity as a result of a policy change. Historical and recent events are about creating the context in which teachers have to get it right. Such an emphasis on problem-solving means that education management products float free of the historical and contemporary policy context. As Blanchard *et al.* (1989) state:

> In this book we do not comment on the appropriateness of introducing LFM: this can be safely left to the politicians, professional associations and, ultimately, the electorate. (p.1)

This echoes Osborne's (1990, p.1) view that having 'the explicit consideration of the broader themes of education management as such is a *luxury* which fewer people will have had the time, or perhaps the inclination, to undertake' (my emphasis). However, the conceptualization of history as a luxury is a necessity for the manufacturing and marketing of education management products. The work of Bell (1992) illustrates how the management of teachers within teams is legitimized through a particular use of historical events. Consider the following:

> Clearly the responsibility for the overall management and administration of every school rests with the headteacher and the senior management team working with and through the governing body. This is immutable and will remain so in spite of the recent changes contained in the 1986 and 1988 Education Acts. Nevertheless, it is becoming increasingly clear that the whole staff of the school is expected to exercise greater collective responsibility for the context of the curriculum, the forms of assessment, the deployment and utilisation of resources, the routine decisions which are taken about children and the ways in which they are to be taught. (p.1)

Bell (1992) uses official documents from the DES and HMI combined with recent legislation to describe the new world in which practitioners now find themselves. Therefore events such as the National Curriculum mean that there has been 'a shift from management by consensus to management by accountability' (p.6) and 'it requires the highest level of management skill *to cope* with these demands' (my emphasis) (p.7). Events provide the teacher with 'challenges' and 'problems' which need 'new sets of understandings and skills' (p.3) and 'solutions'. For Bell (1992), the aims of the National Curriculum 'will not just happen' (p.8), but have to be managed through an understanding of what the management implications are, such as the management of staff and resources. The necessity to work in teams becomes obvious for the reader in the call for 'an examination of the ways in which staff are consulted about the work of the school and are involved in the decision-making, planning and implementation processes in their schools, faculties, departments and teams' (pp.8–9). If there is perspective then it tends to be a clairvoyant role in futuring for the practitioner and speculating on what is waiting round the corner to be the next problem or opportunity. As Bell (1992) confidently states:

> We are now moving into an era when flexible and responsive management of schools is necessary to ensure that new challenges can be met and overcome. (p.10)

Therefore events are used to make generalized statements about the context managers are in, with the direct purpose of ensuring that the reader is (a) convinced that this is how the world looks and you cannot sit around crying 'woe is me' but you have to cope, and (b) the solutions are provided within this product to enable you not just to cope but to improve as well. The use of terms such as 'required', 'accept', 'must' and 'should' means that alternative explanations are not considered and the reader is exhorted to accept the context within which he or she is working. Therefore for Bell (1992):

> ... staff in schools are being required to accept an increased managerial responsibility. To a large extent this is a result of a broad range of policies intended to

increase the effectiveness of the internal management of schools. This found its expression in the legislation affecting schools that was passed in the 1980s concerning teachers' conditions of service, the role of governors in the management of schools, and changes in the ways in which schools are resourced. Some senior managers devote time to resource management and to managing the external relationships of the school, including those mechanisms by which schools have to render themselves accountable. Other staff in the school, therefore, have to accept greater responsibility for its internal management. To do this effectively teams have to be established and developed to cope with a wide range of tasks, or the autonomy of the teacher in the classroom has to give way to a more collegial, co-operative approach to the management of the school. (pp.11–12)

There is no place within this certainty of events and what they mean for alternative explanations. For example, Ball's (1990a) argument based on historical and ethnographic research that the Education Reform Act has brought about a control over teachers' work and has turned the teacher into a technician has no place in the managerialist review of events. Teachers will not buy education management products that claim to deprofessionalize them, and therefore events are structured to make teachers comfortable and even excited by the way legislation and government reports have provided them with new and innovative management opportunities.

Just how pervasive is this limited use of history within the Education Management Industry? You could pick an education management product off your shelves and see for yourself! This is exactly the type of activity or call for action that is evident in a lot of education management products at the end of chapters. For example, at the end of Chapter 1, Bell (1992) asks three questions that require the reader to be a reflective practitioner by considering the impact of changes such as LMS on the individual and the school. The reader is not asked: what is the link between government policy and the promotion of the management model? Furthermore, Bell does not ask himself: why am I a participant within the Education Management Industry? What choices have I made at different times in my career which have led me to advocate the management model? Why am I promoting teams as a solution and does this mean I am collaborating with government policy?

Such historical reflection and reflexivity is generally not evident within education management products. An example of education management products being very busy but historically blind is illustrated by the *Issues in School Management* series of books. There are now nine books in the series covering a range of education management issues: marketing (Davies and Ellison, 1991), school development planning (Davies and Ellison, 1992), quality (West-Burnham, 1992), appraisal (Bennett, 1992), career development (Thody, 1993), legal issues (Adams, 1993), mentoring (Smith and West-Burnham, 1993), inspection (Ormston and Shaw, 1993, 1994), and primary school management (Davies and Ellison, 1994). What is interesting in reading and reviewing these products is the variety of ways in which history is treated by the authors: it can be either totally absent (the usual case), or used (though rarely) to explain educational change.

Bennett (1992) focuses on implementing developmental appraisal effectively within a hostile environment, but does not treat history with the same contempt as do many of the other books in the series. Historical analysis is used to see the origins and debate over control and developmental models and this enables a contradiction between the two trends to be identified within the 1991 regulations on teacher appraisal (DES, 1991). Furthermore, the headteacher's story of appraisal and the unfolding of events within a high school gives recognition to the complexity of change, and how the internal implementation of externally imposed change has to be related to institutional history, culture, and the 'baggage' that is carried through time.

A review of the other texts in the series illustrates the poverty of historical analysis. A basic understanding of the law and where to seek additional advice is the key learning outcome from Adams (1993). This contrasts sharply with the in-depth analysis of the legal context in which education is located by Feintuck (1994), who argues that the law should not be disconnected from the social and political context which generates and implements it.

Often within 'management-by-ringbinder' products historical events are an irritation to be acknowledged and then passed over. This is illustrated by Ormston and Shaw (1994), who 'tell it how it is'; controversy is mentioned but does not hinder the prescriptive bandwagon from rolling on. In relation to the role of parents and inspection Ormston and Shaw (1994) state:

> Parents choose schools, and funding goes to the schools chosen by parents. Thus, the argument goes, parents will drive up standards in schools. Schools deserted by parents, on the other hand, in this simplistic equation, will close through lack of funding. The reality is not quite like this; many pupils are prevented from attending the schools of their parents' choice for a variety of reasons.
>
> Parents will nevertheless play a key role in inspection. Consultation with the parents of the pupils attending a school due for inspection will influence the choice of emphasis when inspectors decide what they will look at particularly. (p.41)

The issues surrounding government policy are acknowledged but quickly passed over in favour of getting on with managing parental involvement in inspection. Therefore the inspection process is disconnected from the historical and contemporary events that are shaped by values, culture and debates about purpose. Other books in the series give recognition to the fact that there are problems: for example, West-Burnham (1992) acknowledges the problems with the transferability of Japanese management models, and Davies and Ellison (1992) note the problems with rational approaches to planning, but there is no in-depth discussion and it is almost as if mere recognition that working in schools isn't easy is enough.

History is often seen as purely factual events that facilitate the promotion of management models. Mountford (1993) provides us with a checklist of events in the development of school-based ITT which leads on to the management imperative central to school–higher education partnerships. For West-Burnham (1992), recent legislation is about challenging the 'established ways' in which schools and teachers do things:

> Historically schools have responded to change in an incremental and piecemeal fashion, gradually assimilating some new requirements, subverting or modifying others and even ignoring a few. The realignment of the education service following the 1988 Education Act in particular makes such responses inappropriate and impractical. Indeed the lack of a coordinated response may well prove to be dysfunctional, not only generating acute internal tensions but questioning the survival of the school itself. The analogy may be drawn with the person planning to take up the game of squash: investing in designer clothing and equipment, reading the rule book and joining the club but not bothering to develop the skills or, crucially, to get fit. A heart attack often results; in order to get fit a diagnosis of the demands to be made on the system is necessary. (pp.1–2)

This diagnosis is more complex than those given by other writers in the same series (Davies and Ellison, 1992), but it is still limited. Events and concerns about social pressures are responded to by a prescription in the form of an exhortation for the need to 'have the knowledge, skills and qualities appropriate to the new situation' (p.4), and furthermore, the danger of managerialism can be prevented by the specific panacea of quality management processes. While the problems of quality are briefly acknowledged, it is the discovery and popularization of it which provides legitimacy. But getting fit is not just a question of having the skills and knowledge as heart attacks are not just the product of mismanaged health but also the product of historical lifestyles and DNA. Hence there are structures (social and biological) that can have an impact on the ability of the individual to get fit, and what medical research can do is to help provide understanding which supports collective and collaborative action.

Bowe *et al.* (1992) are concerned about the link between historical analysis and the management of change. Firstly, the 'single change focus' of many management products is too simplistic, and therefore we see books on appraisal, marketing, inspection and planning as if the change requirements can be seen and managed in isolation. Secondly, there is a neglect of institutional history:

> The assumption, again often unexplained, is that life begins with the moment of innovation, rather than seeing new changes as related to and building upon a history of old ones. Change is set within and is accommodated to the micropolitical history of the institution. Furthermore the history of change in institutions is typically a history of conflict, it is rarely the technical and consensual process that so many organizational theorists portray. (p.141)

Therefore in *Marketing the Secondary School* (Davies and Ellison, 1991) we are told that, 'every school has a reputation and that reputation has to be managed' (p.2), and so the book goes on to provide the ingredients and methods for a successful marketing recipe. A successful relationship between the school and the client is seen to be central, and in order to facilitate this there is a lot of emphasis on 'information' collection. However, history is missing and would get in the way of the certainty of the management strategies. Events, myths, culture, ethos and values are strengths to be built on or must be turned from threats into opportunities. The client is someone who chooses the school; who identifies with the school as a problem-solving forum; who has perceptions and attitudes which are capable of being accessed by attitude surveys. However, an investigation informed by historical analysis might reveal that parental choice is a very complex issue (Feintuck, 1994); we may also be able to consider whether all the problems brought to school every day are educational ones; and furthermore, we might begin to wonder whether survey databases really do encapsulate the truth. In other words, we cannot just control the intake of a school by looking at 'the educational experience which is being offered' (Ellison, 1994, p.4), because communities in which schools are located have histories in which there are social and economic structures that determine the intake. As Bowe *et al.* (1992, p.142) go on to argue, we should not characterize the past as a 'golden age', but neither should we assume that we can 'wipe the slate clean'. Yes, we should challenge what we do and why we are doing it, but with due regard for the complexity in which change takes place.

Jurassic research

The lack of historical analysis and explanation within education management products has implications for research in education management. If we consider for example the work of Caldwell and Spinks (1988, 1992) and Hargreaves and Hopkins (1991), we can see that management strategies advocated within their publications and consultancies/seminars/training sessions have been a product of a research process with practitioners and within educational institutions. The publications aim to describe the management approach such as Collaborative School Management (Caldwell and Spinks, 1988, 1992) and School Development Planning (Hargreaves and Hopkins, 1991) for the practitioner audience and therefore celebrate the dissemination of good practice based on core beliefs and articulated value systems. It is clear from the texts that the widespread popularity and adoption of techniques such as Collaborative School Management illustrates the interest and value attached to this work by practitioners. The encouragement of the reflective practitioner is both recognized and encouraged as a means to securing empowerment and therefore personal and institutional development. As Hargreaves and Hopkins (1991) state:

> It is the nature of development planning that it is not a simple set of practices, techniques or recipes that one school can copy from another. Every school has

to find its own unique approach to development planning; this is essential if there is to be real progress in making the school a more effective and rewarding place for teachers and students. (p.viii)

Therefore development is conceptualized in relation to given assumptions about empowerment as being a 'good thing' and an optimistic and valuable process and end product. What is missing for the practitioner is the opportunity to engage in a historical analysis of where, why and how empowerment has become this accepted management and developmental goal. The reflective practitioner would thus be able to engage in a critical understanding of the processes outlined rather than accept such text as value-free guides for action. In reading such textbooks I am left wanting to know more about some very crucial questions. The authors show the evidence and importance of practitioner involvement in the development, trialling and updating of the techniques and processes, but we are not privy to the discussions and debates about methodology and research processes. The prefaces and acknowledgements are the most fascinating parts of the books and provide a tantalizing glimpse of the research process in action, but it is all presented in such a tidy and concise way that we must accept the inevitability of the techniques outlined. Hargreaves and Hopkins (1991) state:

> We have drawn freely upon the experiences of all who were involved with the project. We do not present any case-studies in the usual sense of that term. We think it more helpful to draw out from a wide range of practices adopted by different schools and LEAs what seem to us both to be the key principles which lie behind the most effective practice and to be some of the dangers which need to be avoided. (p.viii)

Therefore how were the choices made? Did the authors make any errors in the process of selection? Were there conflicts between what can be regarded as good practice? And so on. Caldwell and Spinks (1992) have been quite open in their discussion of amendments and developments within the Collaborative School Management model, but what is not presented is a biographical narrative or account of how they have gone about the process of interacting with their peers, and how they feel about how their values and approaches have changed (or not).

It is becoming increasingly obvious that the mere acknowledgement of the role of practitioners in the development of management products just won't do any longer. This treats course and research participants as informants rather than active research partners within the process. This is not only a denial of the changes that have taken place in the social sciences (see below), but also questions the validity in the process of publishing models and techniques developed in one setting and time context for transference to another. The outcome orientation of the dissemination of good practice within DIY education management guides denies the exploration of the processes which led to that outcome as opposed to another. Furthermore it conscripts (often by default, as dissent is not recorded) practitioners into the process of making government reforms work, and work better. This provides a very poor role model for practitioners and their own research, which, although it has merit and the potential to develop the reflective practitioner, is more often than not concerned with the implementation of externally driven changes. Recent publications (Preedy, 1989; Crawford *et al.*, 1994) of practitioner projects in education management are to be welcomed, especially for the potential partnership between practitioners and researchers in all sectors. However, it is clear that the Education Management Industry is having its effect on practitioner conceptualization of their own and their colleagues' professional development. There is a clear emphasis on getting the management processes right so that we can best cope with external challenges, or so that we can best salvage what is left of our professional discretion and judgement. The ethical issues surrounding the role of the internal and external consultant is frequently noted and often discussed in relation to the issues surrounding the management processes, but there is little acknowledgement of motives or values, or reflection on issues such as professionalism and what the research design shows about their sense of purpose as a professional. Knowledge creation through research by teachers about their own work is not just an issue about the use or uselessness of case study research, but about whether the emphasis on 'know how' and the technical and/or process skills actually moves the practitioner forward as a professional. Literature reviews often seem to be literally searches for the right type of technique (often business techniques such as SWOTs) or theory (often systems theory) rather than an understanding of why they are making the search in the first place, and how the uncritical adoption of business techniques is having an impact on their purpose and role within educational institutions.

There is research and writing within education that can provide the practitioner with access to case studies which enable the development of a broader understanding of what it means to be a teacher/lecturer in educational institutions. The review of case studies as a means of enabling the link between the historical and contemporary policy context and practice at institutional level has been argued by Ozga (1987, 1990) and she notes that the problem is complex and that there has been slow progress. There is evidence of the importance of case studies from the pre- and post-ERA context such as Richardson (1973), Hughes (1974), Goulding *et al.* (1984), Preedy (1989) and Crawford *et al.* (1994) in that they show 'the richness of the picture they presented, and the detail of their description' (Ozga, 1990, p.360), but their limitations are often in the absence of a 'consideration of broader issues, such as what part their detailed account of a specific issue played in the creation of a bigger picture, and what theoretical perspective informed their studies' (Ozga, 1990, p.360).

More recent work has shown the value of case study and its ability to investigate implementation issues within the broader policy-making context. These studies illustrate the limitations of education management products divorced from social science theory and from the bigger picture because they can only provide prescriptions for action rather than critical discourse about the reasons for, and possible consequences of that action. Dale's (1990) study into City Technology Colleges (CTCs) presents a Marxist critique of the state in which education is seen as supporting capital accumulation. What he identifies is a series of changes within what he calls the 'Thatcherite Project' in which there is a contradiction, 'a set of policies and programmes given broad coherence by the attempt simultaneously to "free" individuals for economic purposes but to control them for social purposes' (p.4). In spite of this contradiction, if the CTCs had been set up and operated as intended, then issues such as pedagogy, curriculum, selection of pupils, parental choice and organizational control would have been determined by business management approaches such as production, performance, people as resources, planning and process. However, Dale's research shows that economic liberation has not taken place, as key stakeholders such as industry and parents have not supported the initiative, and therefore the restructuring of education and the survival of CTCs has taken place through government subsidy rather than through the market. This work enables pedagogy, curriculum, pupil selection, parental choice and organizational control to be seen within a strategic context of educational change, whereas education management would be solely concerned with describing and evaluating the operation of pupil recruitment rather than seeing it as a policy mechanism for changing values and behaviours.

Work by Gewirtz et al. (1993) is concerned with examining the impact of market-driven educational provision on a case study school: Northwark Park. The key focus is on the tension between the value system and culture of the school within a marketplace of competition and choice. The main finding is that, 'there is ... a significant mismatch between the established culture of the school and the culture of the market, and the sharpness of this dichotomy produces dilemmas in the school's response' (p.237). What is interesting in this study is that there is a clash between the educational issues of pedagogy and pastoral care within a value system of equity and service, with the new managerialism of school development planning to achieve effective change and resource management based on efficiency and economy. This is apparent in the evidence that Gewirtz et al. (1993) discuss in relation to mixed ability grouping, and in fact becomes very clear over the issue of exclusions. During an in-service day on the school development plan, the staff raise pedagogic issues amidst a forum designed to feedback on a managerialist agenda. This challenge to value systems brought about by policy changes since the 1988 ERA enables us to see that the schools' right-to-manage endemic in education management textbooks and ring-binders is inappropriate. The effective management of the school is dependent on the interaction with the policy context, and what is significant about this case study is the importance of key interest groups connected with the school in holding on to their value system rather than abandoning the values and/or the school.

What these two case studies illustrate is that research must be both busy and observant. The Education Management Industry must take the blame for the denial of historical and contemporary policy issues as being valid areas for exploration and analysis by practitioners.

Jurassic management: beyond entertainment

Historical enquiry is supported by many writers in policy studies, for example, Ball (1990a), Bowe *et al.* (1992), Dale (1989), Ozga (1987), Ozga and Gewirtz (1994), but it is sadly lacking in educational management products which focus on the here and now. The role of history is still regarded as a vibrant and valid approach within education. Silver (1990) argues that:

> History is the recording and analysis of change – when, how and why it took place, or didn't. Historians are not alone in their pursuit – being joined by anthropologists, evaluators, economists and – at times – most social and political scientists. Historians are alone, however, in having the broad processes and detailed accounting of and for change and its absence as their entire occupation. Selecting from and giving real or apparent coherence to the human record is their sole mission. In doing so they join their other social and political science and other partners in imposing order on detail, employing concepts which organize their data, bounding their sequences and selections with the limitations and opportunities of theory and contributing back to it, and using or explicitly formulating strategies of understanding and explanation. (p.1)

Therefore history is more than the collection of facts, and for those historians who claim to ensure that no interpretation is taking place there is a need to investigate at the simplest level: what makes a fact a fact? Interpretation cannot be separated from the process of collection and presentation of historical data. History is relevant to social science in that it enables social scientists to understand and describe contemporary problems, and facilitates comparisons. Social science is relevant to history in providing theory and concepts to help in the presentation and continual revision of interpretation. Therefore, as Mills (1970) has stated,

> More important than the extent to which historians are social scientists, or how they should behave, is the still more controversial point that the social sciences are themselves historical disciplines. (p.162)

Historical analysis can be said to have a number of purposes which will support its relevance to a social science investigation: firstly, Silver (1990) argues that 'History is inevitably ... theoretical' (p.7), and in an earlier work he gives an explanation for this:

> Without the historical test, theory may be beautiful but may be beyond validation and understanding. *Without the theoretical test, history may be busy but blind.*
> (Silver, 1983, p.245) (my emphasis)

In a similar vein, Mills argues for the importance of theory:

> if historians have no 'theory', they may provide materials for the writing of history, but they cannot themselves write it. *They can entertain, but they cannot keep the record straight.*   (1970, p.161) (my emphasis)

What both these writers are illustrating is that theory is important to the historian in enabling understanding and explanation. For example, historians not only have to give meaning but also have to understand meaning associated at different times with different concepts such as bureaucracy, class, state and capitalism. Theory can enable the historian to construct frameworks in which to understand actions and choices by people. Secondly, any interpretation and understanding of current social science issues such as power, markets and social injustice would benefit from a historical perspective by enabling us to see not just how the current situation is, but its antecedence. The study and practice of education which is focused entirely on the here and now is narrow and misleading.

Central to the importance of studying historical material is that of revisionism, and how historians create 'alternative pasts' (Silver, 1990, p.166). Our views of the past are complex and can be shaped by individual and collective agendas. This is more than just myths that grow up about past events and how they shape current social, political and economic activities, but about historiography or the history of historical interpretation. Historians need to give recognition to their own value systems, which inform interpretation and how history is presented:

> like any other form of social or political analysis, history means versions of history, may be radical or conservative, may be engaged in the confident pursuit of a reality or in reassessing the sources of confidence. Historians, social scientists, policy analysts, may tell 'truth to power', but there is no monopoly of the truth to be told.   (Silver, 1990, p.184)

A further perspective on meaning in historical analysis is how it is linked to the future and not just the present. Silver (1990) argues that this future orientation is about methodology in which 'historians trade interpretations which in some way address conceptions of the future' (p.7), and this is further supported by Mills (1970), who asserts that historical investigations should be more than identifying trends and discontinuities: we should not ask 'has something persisted from the past?' but 'why has it persisted?' (p.171). A further issue identified by Mills (1970) is what he calls 'historical specificity' (pp.173–4), in which we need to recognize that not everything comes out of the past and that there are new things, and this affects whether historical explanations have a value. Mills does not advocate a retreat from history; rather there is a plea for comparative studies in which alternatives allow an understanding of historical trends. Furthermore, Silver (1990) argues that it is about process because historians, by virtue of method, order and reorder facts and create meaning, and therefore this tells 'us not only how the historian perceives a reality but how it is possible to perceive it …

The very vocabularies in which historians encapsulate their realities have some kind of intended immortality' (p.7). Versions of the past affect choices about the future and a key issue is not just recognizing the vocabularies that people in a historical context use to describe and give meaning to decisions and their lives, but also how the work of the historian, working in the present but with an eye on the future, is affected by current words and interpretations.

If the Education Management Industry begins to look at its use of history within its products then it might begin to look at its own history as a field of application. Callahan's book *Education and the Cult of Efficiency* (1962) is about 'the origin and development of the adoption of business values and practices in educational administration' (Preface) in the USA 1900–30. In the final chapter, which Callahan calls 'An American Tragedy in Education', he describes the following four developments:

- educational questions were subordinated to business considerations;
- administrators (i.e. managers) were produced who were not, in any true sense, educators;
- a scientific label was put on some very unscientific and dubious methods and practices;
- an anti-intellectual climate, already prevalent, was strengthened. (p.246)

Parallels can be drawn between the USA early this century and the current education system in the UK:

- efficiency and value for money are determining priorities and choices rather than educational issues;
- a survey of the educational press shows that in-service and post-graduate management qualifications put emphasis on training in business management techniques and process;
- the adoption of outcome measures of institutional performance supported by a rational cycle of quality control inspections is being used to make schools more accountable;
- the professional skills, knowledge, and practices of teachers have been ridiculed in order to facilitate right-wing reforms.

Therefore, can we recognize some modern-day relevance in the following comment on the early decades of the twentieth century in the USA?

> Efficiency and economy – important as they are – must be considered in the light of the quality of education that is being provided. Equally important is the inefficiency and false economy of forcing educators to devote their time and energy to cost accounting. We must learn that saving money through imposing an impossible teaching load on teachers is, in terms of the future of our free society, a very costly practice.   (Callahan, 1962, p.263)

Is the Education Management Industry a part of the current tragedy within education in which the new 'cult of efficiency' is being legitimized by their products? Teachers in schools are being subjected to new forms of management control which are dressed up in the rhetoric of participation and empowerment.

A contemporary overview of the Education Management Industry shows that the historiography of the field is patchy and limited in its scope; but its central theme is that of the growth of the management imperative. *Celebratory* studies tend to focus mainly on how far have we come since the early days, and what is it that we have achieved given that British academics and practitioners were 'late arrivals' to the field (Hughes, 1978, p.1). The key people involved tell the stories of the early pioneers of the first courses for educational administrators, the establishment of the British Educational Administration Society (BEAS) in 1971, and those who went out and made connections abroad (Bone, 1982; Hughes, 1974, 1978). The management imperative is celebrated and is seen as an essential professional competence in the management of educational institutions. It is concerned with supporting the practitioner at a time of change in the size of schools, the nature of the secondary school, curriculum reappraisal and the recognition of pupils and parents as clients (Hughes, 1974).

Positional approaches tend to engage in debates about, firstly, issues such as the nature of educational institutions in their similarity to, or difference from, other management settings such as business and industry, and/or educational institutions in other countries; secondly, the transferability and application of theory developed in alternative management settings to educational institutions in England and Wales; and, thirdly, pedagogy within in-service education and professional development in general.

Review approaches tend to be the opportunity for those working and writing in the field of education management to engage in stocktaking, and try to put a rationale or framework on education management as a field of study and its purpose. Such historiography is rare and tends to be in the form of discussion articles (Glatter, 1979), which often preface bibliographies on the mushrooming field in an attempt to understand what education management is and what it is becoming (e.g. Howell, 1978; Harris-Jenkins, 1984, 1985).

Agenda setting or the 'Nostradamus effect' is evident in a range of work on education management, and there seems to be an obligation on education management writers to extrapolate what it is that education managers need to be thinking about as a part of their management and personal development agenda. Davies and Ellison (1994) tell us that 'a little crystal ball gazing may provide practical insights to deal with the growing challenge of the next millennium' (p.x). Bell (1991) identifies an agenda for the 1990s by conceptualizing a number of problems facing academics and practitioners. For academics he identifies three issues:

- the need to develop a more rigorous empirical research and theory base for education management;

- teaching and learning need to be more central rather than the dominance of management as an end in itself;
- management competences are identified by Bell as a 'band-wagon' which is rolling, and he 'suspect(s) will be a major thrust in educational management in the next few years' (p.138).

For the practitioner he identifies six management issues on the agenda:

- endemic change means that management strategies will have to be rethought;
- new working relationships with LEAs, and the broader community;
- the need to develop a marketing strategy;
- human resource development in relation to teacher recruit-ment, retention, and professional development;
- curriculum management will have to make a shift from the managerialism of resource priorities and allocation processes to actual teaching and learning. This is central to institutional development in which 'school development planning and other strategies for ensuring that schools are managed in a coherent, rational and relatively stable way over time, subject to stable resourcing over time, will become part of day-to-day manage-ment of schools' (p.140);
- the importance of quality and the monitoring of standards.

Throughout the article endemic change makes management an imperative, and underpinning the agenda for the academic and the practitioner is the need for stability within a turbulent world in order to let the manager get on with managing.

What this brief overview of the historiography of education management illustrates is that those involved in the field tend to focus on the defence of the management imperative as a means of initially establishing and then maintaining the legitimacy of the field. Education management seems to be so concerned with establishing itself as a legitimate area of study and appli-cation that it has not yet been prepared to engage in an in-depth historical exploration and review itself.

Jurassic management and emancipation

Historical processes would enable the Education Management Industry participants and observers to engage in a reflective and reflexive approach to what they are doing and why they are doing it. For writers within the Education Management Industry to engage in historical inquiry they need to make the value system on which their research is based explicit. This has to be more than the current practice of 'we hold these strategies to be self-evident and they are based on our firm belief in participation, ownership and empowerment' as an exhortation of values explicit in the promotion of particular survival strategies. Rather, values are integral to the choices and actions that education management practitioners and researchers make within the research processes in which they are involved.

Values are not simple statements of belief but are complex issues which provoke debate, uncertainty and questioning. The literature on the education system illustrates heated debates over issues such as the role of the state in policy formulation, in which Neo-Marxists emphasize the importance of the state as a coercive power, while pluralists see the state as a neutral (to varying degrees) referee in policy-making processes. This raises the issue that it is difficult to understand choices, actions and the link between cause and effect, as Silver (1990, p.8) argues:

> Past decisions and policies may appear to have been so, and outcomes may appear to have been identical with intentions. Historians are consistently, however, uncovering the complex and elusive nature of choice and anticipated outcomes, indicating not so much the recipes that have worked as the intangible properties of the ingredients, and their possible or perhaps sometimes probable relationships to one another. In reassessing those past choices historians diminish heroes, reinstate villains, revile previous scholarship for its methodological, substantive or, therefore, theoretical inadequacy.

The growth in post-positivist methodologies such as feminism (Harding, 1987; Hammersley, 1992), anti-racism (Troyna and Williams, 1986), Neo-Marxist (Ozga and Gewirtz, 1994) and emancipatory research (Lather, 1986) provides some rich and fertile ground for education management reflection and reflexivity. As Hesse (1980) has argued:

> ... the attempt to produce value-neutral social science is increasingly being abandoned as at best unrealizable, and at worst self-deceptive, and is being replaced by social sciences based on explicit ideologies, or at least on explicit points of view related to particular interests in society. (p.247)

The critique of the positivist research tradition is focused on a number of issues which all stem from the argument that research cannot be neutral, and following a method does not lead to truth (Lather, 1986, p.259). Social research needs to ask questions about what is happening, what is really happening, and why. In order to do this, the traditional methodologies put forward by Bell (1987) and Cohen and Manion (1980) are too limited in their emphasis on data collection and problem-solving. Post-positive research rooted in critical theory is not concerned with problem-solving within the current framework, but about questioning the status quo. As Cox (1981) has shown, critical theory:

> stands apart from the prevailing order of the world and asks how that order came about. [It] does not take institutions and social and power relationships for granted but calls them into question by concerning itself with their origins and how and whether they might be in the process of changing. (p.129)

In this sense research is recognized for what it is: a social activity; and the link between human action and the research process and learning outcomes is also recognized. This is facilitated by a broader approach to theoretical models and concepts, critical research is not narrow but borrows from the broader social sciences, e.g. from Marxism and feminism (Troyna, 1994a, p.72). Therefore critical research is identified as being emancipatory, and is based on the validation of experience. This is where feelings and experiences cannot be discounted, and there is no real objective evidence. For Stanley and Wise (1983), objectivity is:

> an excuse for a power relationship every bit as obscene as the power relationship that leads women to be sexually assaulted, murdered, and otherwise treated as mere objects. The assault on our minds, the removal from existence of our experiences as valid and true, is every bit as objectionable. (p.169)

Therefore, knowledge production is not a technical activity in which research can reinforce and strengthen existing structures. Neither is it a 'rape model' where the 'career advancement of researchers [is] built on their use of alienating and exploitative inquiry methods' (Lather, 1986, p.261). Hence the research method becomes a metaphor for the research methodology in the empowerment of the researched to participate in the research process and engage in a reciprocal relationship with the researcher. This facilitates validity, and enables consciousness to be developed. Mies (1983) calls this 'conscientisation', in which 'the study of an oppressive reality is not carried out by experts but by the objects of the oppression' (p.126). As Lather (1986) states:

> Emancipatory knowledge increases awareness of the contradictions hidden or distorted by everyday understandings, and in doing so it directs attention to the possibilities for social transformation inherent in the present configuration of social processes. (p.259)

This research process is based on clear ethical principles about the role of the researcher and a rejection of a power-based hierarchical relationship.

Feminist and emancipatory research has been criticized, and in fact among feminist researchers there is an ongoing debate about the researcher–researched relationship, validity and the role of theory. Hammersley (1992), in his discussion about feminist methodology, presents a critique which sums up the key concerns that are often raised:

- the validity of experience might be nothing more than sophisticated navel-gazing;
- the emancipatory process is not as simple as it sounds. A person might be oppressed and an oppressor at the same time; emancipation cannot be a once and for all overcoming of the oppressor, but is more complex. In fact it is argued that the satisfaction of needs has to take into consideration the tension between the individual and the collective – one person's content-

ment is another's concern;

- the research process cannot completely empower the researched as there are certain limitations on the researcher. The researcher has expert knowledge about the research process and knowledge generation.

As Hammersley (1992) states:

> whether we like it or not, researchers necessarily claim some intellectual authority by publishing their findings also carries some important implications for the organisation of research. The other side of the claim to intellectual authority is an obligation on the part of the researcher to ensure that, as far as possible, the information provided is reliable, and this responsibility cannot be shifted on to the people studied. (p.198)

The response of post-positivist researchers to this type of criticism is two-fold: firstly, to directly refute the points made, for example, Hammersley's article is followed by two discussion papers by Ramazanoglu (1992) and Gelsthorpe (1992) in which, among all the points made, it is clear that Hammersley's (1992) critique of feminist methodologies is itself the subject of criticism based on a lack of an explicit reflection by the writer on his value system and what shapes it. As Ramazanoglu (1992) states:

> Hammersley does not seem to see his own place in the research process as a gendered one, and so treats his conception of reason not as an historical construction but as neutral and presumably gender-free. (p.207)

A second approach is to continue to work on developing post-positivist research methods, and in particular the importance of reciprocity. If emancipatory research is to be facilitated, there is a need for an interactive dialogue, and the researcher has to consider what is appropriate disclosure about the intentions of the interview and how his/her own life interacts with that of the researched. Central to the dialogue are the skills of reflection and reflexivity by all participants in the research, and in particular the need for discussion about false consciousness. What is evident from the current literature is that there are examples of researchers providing a reflective account or 'research biographies' (Ball, 1990c) of the research process, and this is complemented by articles discussing the strengths and weakness of this approach. Examples of research biographies are illustrated by Ozga and Gewirtz (1994), in which they discuss the ethical issues in their 'Elites Project' concerning: access issues; a decision not to declare their theoretical orientation; the location of the interviews; personal self-presentation; and how they were compromised as Marxists and feminists. Walford (1994) provides the reader with an account of the research into the Kingshurst CTC in 1987, and his account is about the importance and validity of having a political commitment as a researcher. Troyna (1994a), in giving the account of research into school governing bodies, makes the political commitment of the research team clear:

> In designing and carrying out the project we were mindful of the fact that the research could, indeed should, articulate with our own political activities and struggles as members of local branches of the Labour Party and as school governors based in mainly black, working class institutions. (p.81)

What these three examples illustrate are the key issues being debated in the literature about this approach. Hammersley and Atkinson (1983) have identified the value of research biographies; they

> often have something of a confessional tone to them, whereby the problematic, incomplete, mistaken, dubious, unethical or uncomfortable aspects of the work are allowed to emerge. (p.229)

This is illustrated by the importance of how researchers make such issues as disclosure between the researcher and the researched (see Gordon 1989; McPherson and Raab, 1989) open to peer scrutiny. What is interesting about this approach is that unlike the appraisal interview (see Chapter 3), in which the teacher is encouraged to 'confess' in order to explore doubts and issues as a means of securing a 'fit' with the organizational mission and a consensus value system, the reflexive biography happens within a social science climate in which it is acceptable for researchers to acknowledge and question goals.

Troyna (1994b, p.8) has recognized the importance of this approach, but he questions whether it is of methodological significance. He raises a number of issues. Firstly, that a research biography is no more than 'vanity ethnography' in which only selective excerpts of the research process are given. Secondly, credibility issues involved in research are uppermost when the use of a research biography is currently limited to a small number of sociologists and the mainstream of social science do not use them. In fact, Troyna (1994b) makes the point that research methodology needs to take into account the audience, and that both researchers and those observing, funding and interacting with the research process are sceptical of these types of methodologies. Thirdly, while those who are established in the research industry might feel secure with the process of review and a disclosure of the process, those who are new, such as research students, would find it daunting and therefore it might lead to 'differential power relations between different and competing research paradigms' (p.10). Troyna's (1994b) review of what he identifies as 'taken for granted' assumptions about reflection and self-appraisal is vital in encouraging a debate not so much within sociology – as by his own admission the few who operate it are well versed in the issues – but within the rest of the social sciences. If critical research is to be able to borrow from other disciplines then this relationship must be within itself reciprocal and one of learning. While disclosure to peers might be 'self-selected', the opportunity to question this and triangulate is provided by discussion at conferences and on the pages of learned journals. Furthermore, the questioning of qualitative methods is more a product of the research industry and market: there are the researchers on the one hand and funding agencies on the other. If there is anything that will threaten postgraduates it is not the thought of having to make public the ethical dimension of their research design, but the personal ethical issues of engaging in research which is driven by the market and may not have a purpose beyond 'how to solve' it.

The identification of a post-positivist value system in educational research has certain implications for the Education Management Industry. A glimmer of hope lies in Thody's (1993) preface to *Developing Your Career in Education Management*, in which she gives an account (albeit too brief) of her career path to date in order to illustrate that the book is not '... one of those "do as I say" books or "do as I did" books'. Clearly, narratives and biographies have their place in enabling us to understand our experiences in relation to the 'bigger picture' of macro reforms and change. Gillborn (1994) has the following approach to recent educational legislation and policy initiatives:

> By examining how policy changes are experienced and reconstructed at the micro level we add to our understanding of the processes and dynamics of social change and offer the possibility of more informed, and effective, resistance to those exercises of power that seem likely to widen existing social inequalities. (p.147)

Gillborn's (1994) approach is therefore not just to use questionnaires, semi-structured interviews and observation in order to describe the effective and efficient implementation of externally driven change, but to understand and explain the 'cumulative effects of the several "reforms" bundled together with Conservative education legislation'. What is presented is a clear understanding of the importance of institutional history, culture, patterns and networks of professional relationships, combined with a value system rooted in 'progressive approaches'. This confirms Ball's (1987, 1990a) and Bowe *et al.*'s (1992) work on the importance of micro-political activity and how practitioners actively seek 'spaces' where micro-interpretation of macro policy takes place (White and Crump, 1993, p.426). Therefore teacher behaviour cannot be characterized in terms of good or bad management. Rather, as Gillborn (1994) goes on to argue, the power issues involved need to be seen in relation to the broader context. In particular, the implementation of policy is very complex:

> Macro changes in education policy do not automatically translate into changes at the school level. However, we should not fall into the trap of assuming that such macro changes only alter part of an otherwise fixed equation, as if the chances of change can be calculated if we know enough about other relevant variables ... And yet teacher's values and the culture of a school might come to mean different things in the new reality of radical macro level changes. In addition, variables that were not part of the equation before, might suddenly become crucial as a result of the macro level changes. (p.162)

Studying change within an institutional context has to be more than installing management structures (e.g. teams, vision and mission, integrated staff development); rather social, and in this instance economic, structures brought about change. All that managerialism would have done is to delude the participants into feeling good about it.

What this case study presented by Gillborn (1994) allows us to see is the irrelevance of the 'management by ringbinder' prescriptions, even with the usual 'small print' disclaimer that all schools are different anyway. For White and Crump (1993), Ball's (1990a) work illustrates that

> ... policy is not static, is constantly shifting and, as a process, it is not ever an end product. The cyclical nature of the policy-making process may be established as soon as the intended policy is passed on to those for whom it is intended (in this case the schools and those who work there as staff, students and interest groups). There is no guarantee, however, that this will be identified or that it will occur naturally. Conflict, between macro- and micro-levels of development and from within each level, becomes a part of that cycle. Ideological, epistemological and philosophical discrepancies become enmeshed in the policy text and interpretation. Self-interest and interests of political survival are also involved. (p.425)

The installation of management structures denies the validity of institutional and personal histories, or what Ball calls 'folk knowledge' (White and Crump, 1993, p.426). Methods to control teachers through management ideologies are clearly an additional attempt to prevent policy being fudged, diverted and hindered by the residues of the authentic reflective practitioner.

Therefore, the presentation of prescriptive management strategies with a clear focus that they can and do solve educational problems is in doubt. The argument is that the voices of the participants which led to the construction of the diagrams, proformas, checklists and case studies are not being heard. Furthermore, if the certainty and tidiness within the process which produced the ringbinder or the model is cracked open then a different story could be told through the use of life histories and narratives. This type of research tends to be used in feminist research in which the accounts of women in subordinate positions are used to challenge the hegemony of dominant accounts. We may therefore be able to see how teachers have grappled with the deficit view of much management training and developmental activities in the promotion of management competences at the expense of professional skills and knowledge. We may also be able to see how participants in the Education Management Industry are able to investigate their place in the management hegemony integral to education policy. From this we might see a dawning recognition that the purpose of education research is about a different type of change management. That is, it is not just about finding out how well we have or have not implemented government policies but also about how to 'harness that analysis to an explicit political commitment to change things' (Troyna, 1994a, p.72).

CHAPTER 5

Chaotic reflexivity

Consider the following extract from a book on leadership and management:

> This is not a book of conclusions, cases, or exemplary practices of excellent
> companies. It is deliberately *not* that kind of book, for two reasons. First, I no
> longer believe that organizations can be changed by imposing a model devel-
> oped elsewhere. So little transfers to, or even inspires, those trying to work at
> change in their own organizations. Second, and much more important, the new
> physics cogently explains that there is no objective reality out there waiting to
> reveal its secrets. There are no recipes or formulae, no checklists or advice that
> describe 'reality'. There is only what we create through our engagement with
> others and with events. Nothing really transfers; everything is always new and
> different and unique to each of us.   (Wheatley, 1994, p.7)

How long will it be before an education management product on leadership and management in educational institutions will have such a reflective
process both at the beginning and throughout? What Wheatley (1994)
records in her book is not just an explanation of the 'new physics' but the
impact it has had on her thinking and her practice as a management
consultant. Such a process can be stimulated by life event(s), interaction
with another person or persons and/or reading influential book(s) or
article(s). The preface of this book shows that for me it was all three, for
Wheatley (1994) it was the reading of Capra's *The Turning Point*, and for
Lewin (1992), *Life at the Edge of Chaos* is more meaningful as a result of
visiting Chaco Canyon and the rainforest.

The process of reflection and reflexivity is essential to learning. We could
ask: what effect does your subject specialism have on your view of the world,
your value systems and, ultimately, what and how you engage in a consultancy or an INSET activity? Wheatley (1994) notes the dominance of engineers
as actual or role models for strategic management theorists, and yet we very
rarely see acknowledgement of these ontological and epistemological foundations of their work. Does being a physicist mean that you generate a
different type of education management product to a social scientist? This
book is about sharing with you the various critiques of education management as a part of encouraging a debate about the Education Management
Industry. This chapter in particular is about asking you to engage in the

reflective and reflexive process and to dig deeper than we have gone so far. By getting in touch with the scientific roots of education management we may even touch some raw nerves within the social sciences in general.

Participants within the Education Management Industry could engage in a process of reflection and reflexivity through the use of Chaos Theory. What is interesting here is the adoption and use of the term Chaos Theory, which in scientific and research circles is known as non-linear dynamics. If this book was in a 'management-by-ringbinder' publication then the title would be there, and as long as I made my value system clear by a statement on the first loose-leaf page, then you the reader would be quite happy to accept or reject on this basis. It is more complex than this, as my adoption of Chaos Theory rather than non-linear dynamics is central to the core themes of this book, i.e. the link between theory and practice and research and practice. This point has been illustrated by Hayles (1990):

> 'chaos theory' and the 'science of chaos' are not phrases usually employed by researchers who work in these fields. They prefer to designate their area as nonlinear dynamics, dynamical systems theory, or, more modestly yet, dynamical systems methods. To them, using 'chaos theory' or the 'science of chaos' signals that one is dilettante rather than an expert. (p.8)

Hayles (1990) goes on to argue that she will use Chaos Theory, as it encapsulates her research process and interests as 'part of my project is to explore what happens when a word such as "chaos", invested with a rich tradition of mythic and literary significance, is appropriated by the sciences and given a more specialized meaning'. For me, this debate illustrates how the use of words and labels can be significant in understanding the struggles over status, knowledge and what is defined as intellectual rigour. A key critique of this book could be that I am operating in the very 'management-by-ring-binder' mode that I am worried about. Dipping into science theory in order to provide a strategy for education management to get itself out of the hole it has dug itself into is hardly legitimate when my critique is based on the consumerist approach behind the content of many education management products. The simplest defence might be to say that I had to use education management approaches in order to be bought, read and understood. This would be partronizing, unproductive and incorrect. The answer lies within an aspect of education management history and writings. Education management is generally regarded in the UK as a field of application rather than a discipline (Glatter, 1972, p.51). As Harries-Jenkins (1984) has stated:

> we are looking at a field of management studies characterised by a considerable flexibility of discipline boundaries. A major feature of this has always been the exceptional permeability of these boundaries, so that the development of research and theory in this context has long relied on the work of scholars in such established disciplines as economics, political studies, psychology, and sociology. (p.215)

This echoes the writings of Baron and Taylor (1969), Glatter (1972, 1979), Bone (1982) and Hughes (1978) and gives perspective to the tensions in the development of education management as a field of application. Hughes (1978) argues that a field of application is concerned with 'showing aware-ness and sensitivity in relation to the problems and concerns of the practitioners who provide the justification of the whole enterprise' (p.10). In this way the writings of the scientific movement (e.g. Taylor, 1911, and Fayol, 1916) were close to the practitioner, but too restricted in scope; the phenomenologists put emphasis on the individual in the field in their inter-pretation of the management context; and the Theory Movement turned away from the practical application to develop a general theory of adminis-tration. Hughes (1978) goes on to argue that currently the best way to understand a field of application is by the use of an analogy with medicine:

> Medical Science is a body of knowledge, the elements of which are drawn select-ively from a number of sources on the basis of their relevance to clinical practice. These elements are derived from sub-disciplines of the natural sciences, Physics, Chemistry and Biology and also from clinical experience; the knowledge is organised about problems of practice. From such a viewpoint an understanding, co-operative relationship between a clinician and the analyst, i.e. between the practitioner and the academic, is seen as all-important. (p.10)

Within this framework, the practitioner or clinician communicates with the analyst or academic on what is needed; and the analyst/academic can provide an overview and direction to the clinician/practitioner's work. Therefore practitioner demand and the articulation of problems within education led to a response from academics in the form of courses and research. Academics then turned to theoretical concepts and models in the social sciences in order to meet the need:

> It was the field of practice which presented the problem and provided the initial stimulus, the research itself required an analysis of concepts drawn from the social sciences, the final outcome was to make some contribution, it is hoped, to improve practice (any small contribution to further theory development being an additional bonus). (Hughes, 1978, p.11)

What the theory–practice and academic–practitioner divide is about is status: is a field of application as distinct from a pure discipline or a body of knowledge of a lower status? Hughes (1978) argues that

> the precise boundary between the pure and the applied may be hard to deter-mine, and the traffic in inspiration, ideas and techniques moves in both directions. I therefore have little sympathy with the view sometimes expressed that an applied science is a somewhat inferior form of knowledge to which the high academic standards of the pure disciplines do not apply. When I hear such remarks I almost wish that the phrase 'applied science' had never been invented. (p.13)

Agreed! But since Hughes (1978) wrote those wise words it is clear that they have not been listened to, as evidence of a two-way traffic is absent in the business of education management products. We are all concerned in education with the same issues, and while the focus may be different for some, the key issue is whether such specificity becomes blinkered. The theory–practice divide is a false dichotomy and, as I have said earlier, the justification of this statement has to be more than a debate about the amount and type of practitioner experience which dominates much education management writing.

An interesting way of moving this issue forward is to consider how and why we label social processes. Empowerment, discourse, vision and other popular words would benefit from an understanding of what they really are about and how they could/should be utilized. There are no agendas within this book; if I call Chaos Theory by that title it is not because I am appealing to the common and populist mode but because the title furthers our understanding. I agree that I could be labelled a 'dilettante' as I am not a professional scientist ('O' level biology, grade 5, 1974), but I don't have to be an expert in science in order to gain an understanding of the science foundations to my subject expertise. Subject boundaries are an artificial creation that has more to do with power and exclusivity than it has to do with knowledge creation. I am not consuming scientific concepts in order to promote a management solution, but rather looking at how science can illustrate the failure of such solutions. We learn by analogy, and the use of metaphor triggers recognition and imagination. I will therefore talk about Chaos Theory not as part of an amateur–expert struggle, but because it best describes the scientific processes in which all our work is rooted. How ideas are presented is essential to our work as it enables it to be inclusive or exclusive, and nowhere is this better illustrated than in how science and scientists are presented in the media, and how stereotypes act as barriers to what science is really about and its importance to everyday life. Technical terms like the Latin names for plants are something that the so-called 'amateur gardener' finds of interest as well as the expert. They are part of a shared language in which words, labels and descriptions, when challenged by all participants, facilitate communication, understanding and an appreciation of the plurality of work context and outcomes. Do you know why you use words and phrases like cost effectiveness, efficiency, accountability and delegation? Do you challenge your use of them and consider whether and why you have been co-opted into the language and therefore the ideology of management? The education profession is an educated profession, but why do we persist in educating professionals to do, rather than to think? As Inglis (1985) has powerfully argued:

> The deadly banalities of the management consultant and the technocratic expert are universally deployed to justify arbitrary closure, redundancy, the dereliction of building (plant, as they say), as well as the gross, philistine and self-seeing foreshortening of a humane education. We all of us have innumerable such stories to tell. But through it all, with unshakeable self-satisfaction, the managerialists pursue their unimpeded way, entitling new courses 'the management of contraction', 'the organization of decline', or most risible of all,

'falling rolls'. The inanity of the disciplinary diction should have been enough to kill it off. Stuck with a latter-day and pretentious account of the policy sciences as being capable of bringing about rational progress and the accurate predictions which would permit this consummation, no senior manager ever has recourse to such traditional concepts as wisdom, sagacity, utter accident, sainthood, passion, tragedy, historical understanding. No curriculum advises middle managers to pick at random from Hegel, Turgenev, Dickens, Kierkegaard, Einstein, the Buddha, Aristotle, Prince Kropotkin, Hannah Arendt, Rosa Luxemburg, Chinua Achebe. (pp.105–6)

No education management product asks practitioners to look at the history of science and how it enables us to understand and explain current thinking and practice in a range of fields including management. Chaos Theory can explain why we cannot predict outcomes for some complicated systems like the weather, or earthquakes, or gambling. Chaos Theory is a fundamental paradigm shift and challenges the foundations on which our lives and work are based. Our view of the world is rooted in the natural sciences, and further study illustrates that this is based on the seventeenth-century Newtonian legacy. Let us consider that Kogan (1979) argues

that it is the task of social scientists to take things apart. I assume that it is the task of politicians and administrators to make sure that things are brought back together again ... (p.8)

Such an approach is based on the world as a well-ordered and predictable machine: things can be taken apart, analysed and put back together again without damage. By separating out knowledge into subjects in places of learning, or organizations into departments and roles, we assume that we can understand the whole by investigating the part. Turbulence and disturbance to the system is therefore negative, and a problem. In this world, the emphasis is on either rising above the practical and being characterized as thinkers, or for the practitioner keeping the machine running smoothly, and solving problems. You either do or do not get your hands dirty. Chaos is literally 'chaotic': the imperative is to control change in order to prevent entropy. As Wheatley (1994) has said:

Machines wear down; they eventually stop ... This is a universe, we feel, that cannot be trusted with growth, rejuvenation, process. If we want progress, then we must provide the energy, the momentum, to reverse decay. By sheer force of will, because we are the planet's consciousness, we will make the world hang together. We will resist death. (p.17)

Education management products are designed on seventeenth century assumptions with an emphasis on managerialist techniques and systems, and creating a fear of understanding human relationships. Human resource management, in spite of the rhetoric of empowerment, ownership and collegiality, is still based on control, stability, order and the equilibrium of organizational fit with the environment. This is not a denial that Newtonian physics does not have validity (Toffler, 1984), and as Lewin

(1992) has argued, getting a human to the moon and back is based on the laws of motion and predictability which can be simulated and tested. However, it is time to acknowledge non-linearity in the natural and social world. As Sungaila (1990b) has argued, we cannot allow scientific revolutions to pass us by unnoticed, rather we are alive and we should conceptualize the universe accordingly:

> Machines are not natural. They are not alive. Our world is both. Our students, our schools, our school systems, are alive. So are our language, our culture, our society. Our systems of thought, including our discipline of educational administration, are living systems too. And science has at last begun to grasp the basic principles on which living systems operate. They are self-renewing and self-organizing. (p.6)

This has implications for research and we may compare the act of taking things apart with the implications of Schroedinger's cat for the social scientist. A cat is placed in a box and no one can see inside it. Poison or food can be released at any time; the probability of food or poison is 50:50. When the release mechanism goes, what is the cat's fate? We do not know until we look, and therefore the act of observation creates the cat's situation, '... it is impossible to say that the cat is living or dead until we observe it ... Before we peer in, the cat exists as probabilities. Our nosiness determines its fate' (Wheatley, 1994, pp.59–60).

What this illustrates is that there is a different type of knowledge if we stop investigating on the basis of objective reality. The world of the observer and observed, researcher and researched has been shattered. Furthermore, the Newtonian machine view of the universe elevated humans as a part of a rational process separate from nature. We have lost touch with a respect for the earth and in the late twentieth century we now have the opportunity to revisit that culture, not just through ecology, but through a different understanding of control. As Prigogine and Stengers (1984) have argued, science is more than 'manipulating nature, but it is also an attempt to understand it, to dig deeper into questions that have been asked generation after generation' (p.291). We have spent the last three hundred years trying to prove that natural and social are different, but as Sungaila (1990b) has shown, 'it is now discovered, that the same dynamics underpin *both* natural *and* social life' (p.7; italics in original). Quantum mechanics is a world of discovery rather than scientific method. Particles are not objects, things, items or units which are independent of each other. Relationships are what matter. A particle exists and can only be seen in connection with something else.

Therefore, the closed system of the Newtonian machine has been challenged by the open system in which continued existence is through the constant exchange of energy with the environment. Within closed systems things can be determined and events reversed, but within open systems:

> The irreversibility of such systems implies that they have histories and that they evolve. Discussing an open system then must involve some description of the historical development of the system.   (Sawada and Caley, 1985, p.14)

The message for education management is loud and clear. We have seen real history does not figure much in education management products as they assume that open systems can be subjected to the predictive control mechanisms, reversibility processes and determination of the clock and machine.

Hayles (1990) has identified two different emphases in Chaos Theory which is tied up in the complexity of: there is order within chaos, and there is order out of chaos. Firstly, there is the work of Prigogine, who with Stengers wrote *Order out of Chaos* (1984), and argued that chaos and order are not opposites. Prigogine's Nobel Prize (1977) work on dissipative structures shows how certain chemical processes can lead to self-organization. As energy dissipates the system does not die, but rather there is a regenerative and self-renewing process taking place:

> open systems have the possibility of continuously importing free energy from the environment and of exporting entropy. They don't sit quietly by as their energy dissipates. They don't seek equilibrium. Quite the opposite. To stay viable, open systems maintain a state of non-equilibrium, keeping the system off balance so that it can change and grow. They participate in an active exchange with their world, using what is there for their own renewal. Every organism in nature, including us, behaves in this way. (Wheatley, 1994, p.78)

The system is autopoetic, in which there is a drive for renewal. The system has a boundary that both identifies distinction and integration with the environment, and so I am not a single entity isolated in space but part of a turbulent living network in which I am both individual and social. Therefore, as Toffler (1984, p.xv) argues, '... surely biological and social systems are open, which means that the attempt to understand them in mechanistic terms is doomed to failure.'

A second emphasis in Chaos Theory is about order within chaos or what has been known as 'bounded instability'. This is based on the work of Lorenz, and what are known as 'strange attractors' (see Gleick, 1987, p.90). Hayles (1990) describes this as:

> Whereas truly random systems show no discernable pattern when they are mapped into phase space, chaotic systems contract to a confined region and trace complex patterns within it. The discovery that chaos possesses deep structures of order is all the more remarkable because of the wide range of systems that demonstrate this behavior. They range from lynx fur returns to outbreaks of measles epidemics, from the rise and fall of the Nile River to eye movements in schizophrenics. (pp.9–10)

Therefore order within chaos enables us to consider the 'strange attractors' within organizations, and not just computer modelling. For Wheatley (1994), a potent strange attractor is *meaning*, in which individuals in hostile environments are able to ask and find answers to 'why?':

> If we search to create meaning, we can survive and even flourish. In chaotic organizations, I observed just such phenomenon. Employees were wise enough to sense that personal meaning-making was their only route out of chaos. In some ways, the future of the organization became irrelevant. They held onto personal coherence because of the meaning attractor they created. Maybe the organization didn't make sense, but their lives did. (pp.134–5)

While there is debate among chaos theorists, it is possible to identify some features (Hayles, 1990; Griffiths *et al.*, 1991) of chaotic systems that enable us to gain a different understanding of social processes. Firstly, systems are *non-linear*, in that cause and effect are distant. A small cause can have a large effect, and *sensitivity to local conditions* (butterfly effect) can *amplify* the input through *feedback* loops. Therefore the flap of a butterfly's wings could cause a thunderstorm in another part of the world:

> For small pieces of weather ... any prediction deteriorates rapidly. Errors and uncertainties multiply, cascading upward through a chain of turbulent features, from dust devils and squalls up to continent-sized eddies that only satellites can see.   (Gleick, 1987, p.20)

Secondly, systems are *complex*, and different approaches to scale and measurement are needed. A coastline cannot be measured in the same way as a triangle in which there is an instrument and a precise process based on the truth and accuracy of objective scales and numbers. Mandlebrot's fractals are patterns which are *self-similar* in that they look the same or similar on every scale or dimension in which they are examined.

Chaos Theory has been applied in science to astronomy, physiology, demography, mathematics and meteorology, and within the field of economics some interesting work has been done by Curtis (1990) and Radzicki (1990). The applicability to the social sciences is a matter of dispute. Percival (1991) has argued that:

> Science takes words and shapes their meanings to its own ends, and 'chaos' is no exception. The state of Lebanese politics and British education may look chaotic, but you cannot study them using chaos theory. (p.16)

We may well ask: why not? Recently, writers have begun to recognize the validity of Chaos Theory to social processes within organizations and are moving away from the usual way of seeing 'chaos' and 'the crucial turn comes when chaos is envisioned not as an absence or void but as a positive force in its own right' (Hayles, 1990) . Therefore, Gleick (1987) has argued:

> Now that science is looking, chaos seems to be everywhere ... Chaos appears in the behavior of the weather, the behavior of an airplane in flight ... No matter what the medium, the behavior obeys the same newly discovered laws. That realization has begun to change the way business executives make decisions about insurance, the way astronomers look at the solar system, the way political theorists talk about the stresses leading to armed conflict ... Chaos breaks across the lines that separate scientific disciplines. (p.5)

Books and articles are appearing in which Chaos Theory has influenced the thinking of the writer (Ferchat, 1990; Nilson, 1995), and some interesting analysis has been done by Nonaka (1988), who uses self-organization as a means of understanding and creating self-renewal in Japanese business. Most work has been located within the business sector by Stacey (1991, 1992, 1993), in challenging the orthodoxy of strategic management and using Chaos Theory to illustrate how successful companies achieve by using instability to innovate. Also recommended is the excellent reflexive study by Wheatley (1994) on how Chaos Theory can enable our understanding of leadership to develop through conceptualizing organizations differently:

> If organizations are machines, control makes sense. If organizations are process structures, then seeking to impose control through permanent structure is suicide. If we believe that acting responsibly means exerting control by having our hands into everything, then we cannot hope for anything except what we already have – a treadmill of effort and life-destroying stress. (p.23)

For Wheatley, the lessons of quantum mechanics are clear for organizations, and as a consultant her focus has shifted, 'now I look carefully at how a workplace organizes its relationships; not its tasks, functions, and hierarchies, but the patterns of relationship and the capacities available to form them' (p.39).

In education there is no equivalent to Stacey and Wheatley, but as we have seen, there is a growing disquiet about managerialism in the critique of site-based management. Within the broader field of education management text books we do find the work of Weick (1988) and Cohen and March (1989), in which the reality of the world of rational and costed plans, job descriptions and evaluation schedules is questioned. Weick argues that organizations are 'loosely coupled', while Cohen and March identify the American college and university as 'organized anarchies' in which decision-making can be best understood as a 'garbage can':

> A key to understanding the processes within organizations is to view a choice opportunity (an occasion on which an organization is expected to produce a decision) as a garbage can into which various problems and solutions are dumped by participants. The mix of garbage in a single can depends partly on the labels attached to the alternative cans; but it also depends on what garbage is being produced at the moment, on the mix of cans available, and on the speed with which garbage is collected and removed from the scene. (p.111)

What is interesting is that this world is not reflected in education management products, otherwise the 'recipes' and 'maps' would not produce the solutions. Even within mainstream education management writings there is some difficulty. Weick (1988, pp.61–2) admits to a 'neutral, if not mildly affectionate stance towards the concept' of loose coupling but does acknowledge that it could be met with hostility. We may wonder why in spite of Bell's (1989) argument that hierarchy with vertical and horizontal divisions should be abandoned there is still an emphasis on management control through, for example, teams to deal with issues of 'problematic goals', 'unclear technology', and 'fluid participation' within organized anarchies (Weick, 1988). The drive for stability and consensus is strong for those who present ambiguity models within the mainstream literature. Weick (1976) is quoted by Bush (1995) as follows:

> If there is a breakdown in one portion of a loosely coupled system then this breakdown is sealed off and does not affect other portions of the organisation ... when any element misfires or decays or deteriorates, the spread of this deterioration is checked in a loosely coupled system ... A loosely coupled system can isolate its trouble spots and prevent the trouble from spreading. (pp.116–17)

Disorder is conceptualized as negative and has to be managed. Bush (1995) is concerned that management accountability means that this disorder cannot be tolerated: 'action must be taken to remedy the weakness if the institution is to thrive in a period of heightened market and public accountability' (p.117).

These issues are reflected in other debates over organizational structure and behaviour. Turner (1977) is prepared to argue in favour of educational institutions as 'unpredictable, anarchic organizations with no clear boundaries and a turbulent environment' (in Westoby, 1988, p.83) but his co-writer is concerned with accountability. As Packwood (1977) states:

> The hierarchy, through its properties of accountability and authority, is a rational attempt to combine the activities of many in securing desired ends. Without accountability the organization runs as 'catch as catch can' and any outcome depends upon the power of the individuals concerned. Education is too important for that and it cannot solely depend upon short-term decisions. The result would be unhappy, uneducated children and unhappy, frustrated staff. (in Westoby, 1988, p.84)

In replying, Turner (1977) begins to touch on chaotic issues of how a context is conceptualized. If we want line-managed accountability then we must structure accordingly, but if we see the importance of relationships and information flows then the accountability becomes one of professional dialogue and partnership. While this type of discussion is clearly evident within the broader education management literature, what is missing is that ambiguity and organized anarchy are not taken a stage further by considering how disorder can lead to a positive process of creative self-renewal.

Clearly we have to come to terms with whether the pure excitement and enthusiasm for Chaos Theory makes it just a novelty, and it is open to abuse. In the battle for recognition and consecration within the field of education management, language and specialist terminology could be used to exclude people. All the work currently being done on Chaos Theory illustrates that it is not a bandwagon that is rolling through like Total Quality Management and Competences, but is fundamental to understanding social and educational processes. In Australia, Sungaila (1990a) has argued that there is an 'emerging synthesis in the natural and social sciences' (p.6), and therefore educational observers and practitioners cannot ignore the transformation in science and its applicability to understanding educational systems. Furthermore, work by Snyder *et al.* (1995) based at the University of Florida challenges the 'utility of a linear construct of planned change ...' and contends that, 'Chaos Theory provides a useful mental model of guiding change as leaders garner the energy from unpredictable events for realizing transformation goals' (p.2). In spite of all the books and training on how to plan, structure and identify objectives for a quality teaching and learning strategy we are all aware of the creative process within the classroom and that it is definitely not linear; cause and effect are often not closely related. This is nowhere better illustrated than in concerns being raised about the OFSTED inspection process in England and Wales, where Russell (1994) has argued that the inspection framework is a systems approach which 'is not only conceptually opposed to randomness and maverick creativity. If applied really well it leaves no room for the serendipity that may inspire excellence' (p.311). Hence even though very able and knowledgeable people may be involved in the inspection process, the report may fail to bring about school improvement because, 'to inspire the effort needed in schools to bring about change there has to be that "ah ha" of recognition when the report is read' (p.313). Cziko (1989) has raised questions about educational research based on the rational and predictive certainties of Newtonian physics. He uses the butterfly effect to question the linearity of learning and progression rooted in current educational structures:

> The butterfly effect of chaotic phenomena constitutes a particularly vexing curse for psychometricians because no matter how reliable and valid a test may be, identical scores on a pretest will inevitably lead to unpredictable differences on posttest of later achievement. (p.19)

This clearly has messages for much value-added and school improvement research. For Cziko (1989), in social science research:

> We must, however, always guard against the temptation to make hard and fast predictions of human behaviour and devise 'cookbook' solutions to problems based on our understanding because, as argued here, it is a serious error to believe that one can predict the future based on what has happened in the past.
> Though such research might (indeed, *should*) lead to the implementation and dissemination of innovative educational practices, it must be realized that regardless of the extent of prior research, accurate prediction of outcomes is not possible, and so continuous monitoring and fine-tuning is essential to any educational undertaking. (p.23)

Cziko's paper has provoked debate in the form of a reply by Lehrer *et al.* (1990), in which they question whether behaviour is always indeterminate, and therefore it 'does not mean that behavior is not predictable *within certain tolerances*. The challenge for a theory is to specify these tolerances' (p.17). What would be interesting for the Education Management Industry is to examine how the 'tolerances' have been very narrowly defined to the techniques and language of management, and how a reflective and reflexive process from within the sciences may facilitate challenge and review.

Griffiths *et al.* (1991) recognize that their 'foray into chaotic modeling is a bit "quick and dirty" because of the limitations on data and case construction and the post hoc character of the analysis', but they are positive about the appeal of Chaos Theory and its 'explanatory value' (p.447). However, they are sceptical about it in relation to data collection and research design: if we search for 'strange attractors' then we will find them. Furthermore, the predictive abilities of Chaos Theory are just as limited as what is already available within the social sciences. If we are in search of truth in the tradition of Newtonian physics then so be it, but, as Cziko (1989) argues, the kind of educational research which should take place is one which

> would involve a change from the orthodox 'scientific' research perspective that attempts to predict and control to one that attempts 'only' to describe, appreciate, interpret, and explain the social and individual behaviours as well as the cognitive processes relevant to understanding educational phenomena. Educational research from such a perspective would be essentially descriptive, with useful units of study varying from the macro level of community, school, and classroom to the more micro level of individual behaviors, feelings, and cognitive processes. (p.23)

However, even though valuable work has started in the application of Chaos Theory to the educational context, the relevance may not be immediately clear. For the manager–practitioner schooled in the entrepreneurial mind-set, the science of fractals, strange attractors and the butterfly effect seem far removed from organizational behaviour. Chaos Theory presents the view that to be successful a school or college needs to recognize that educational institutions are not linear but complex networks with equally complex feedback loops. Current orthodoxy is that schools and colleges operate a rational cycle of review, forecast, implementation and evaluation in relation to resource management. Therefore, curriculum and resource needs are identified and prioritized, and forecasts are made of pupil/student numbers and income linked to targets. This is informed by the development plan and the long-term vision of where the school/college wants to be at a given point in the future. During the annual cycle, negative feedback (e.g. changes to the funding formula) is prevented from causing a downward spiral or vicious cycle by monitoring, and adjustments are made in order to ensure stability. Similarly, positive feedback (e.g. increased demand for places in the sixth form) can form a virtuous cycle of success and must be prevented from leading to disintegration or 'explosively unstable equilibrium' (Stacey, 1992, p.62).

The drive for stability is a product of a retrospective view of education and of the perceived need to return to the golden age when the long-term was predictable and all you had to do was to teach. At the core of much management training is the view that managers' concerns must be met by giving them the handbook containing the strategies and tools which will enable stability to return once again to schools and colleges. We see courses about controlling change by adopting the management tools of strategic management, quality management and business planning, combined with stress and self-esteem courses to help managers deal with the guilt and angst when they don't work (Stacey, 1992).

Chaos Theory presents education managers with a third choice to either stability or disintegration, and that is to operate within 'bounded instability' (Stacey, 1992, p.21). A successful school or college would operate away from equilibrium between stability and disintegration. Management behaviour is therefore operating in an environment of constant order and disorder. The future cannot be visioned as it is unpredictable and depends on chance. Feedback can produce behaviour that is complex, in which a direct link between cause and effect cannot be seen. For Bowe *et al.* (1992) the complexity, speed and contradictory aspects of the change process 'make a mockery of the neat and trite prescriptions offered in many of the "how-to-do-it" management texts written to cash in on the ERA reforms' (p.166). Therefore the future is created by the sensitive response to fluctuations in the environment rather than proactive and systematic installations of new structures and tasks. Perhaps education management products require new prescriptions: managers should not be following the John Major call to go 'back to basics', in which history determines the future, nor should the manager yield to the idealism of visioning and let some picture of a desired future determine what you do today. What Chaos Theory enables the manager to do is to explore the issues in relation to what is happening now and recognize the choices from which the future will unfold. Sullivan's (1994) work has shown the importance of human relationships, and how systems co-evolve by a creative process of policy and organizational modification.

Teachers need not panic. The day-to-day issues are within control, it is the long-term issues that have the potential to use a creative or an extraordinary management approach using a chaotic perspective (Stacey, 1992). Furthermore, the future is not random in the ordinary sense of chaos in that it is 'bounded instability'. The weather patterns are not predictable, but they are within a boundary of, for example, the seasons. We might not be able to predict if there will be sun during the Wimbledon tennis championships, but we can recognize patterns and therefore predict that there will not be snow! If it were to snow we would be able to see that each snowflake is unique as a result of fluctuations in the environment in which it was created, but we would also see 'self-similarity' in that the flakes of frozen water can be categorized as snowflakes (Stacey, 1991).

What does the challenge of Chaos Theory mean for the Education Management Industry? The fundamental issue that the Education Management Industry has to grapple with is a confusion between order and control (Wheatley, 1994), and Hargreaves's (1995) critique of Chaos Theory illustrates this. Hargreaves (1995) is rooted in a Newtonian view of the world and so the drive for observable control mechanisms is strong in order to maintain stability and meet the needs and wants of parents and children. 'Corrective control' (p.220) in relation to 'targets, success criteria, action plans, and progress checks' is both possible and desirable through the working of open and closed feedback loops. For Hargreaves, monitoring and evaluation are as essential for whole institutional development as they are for effective teaching and learning. Buried within the article (p.225) is an analysis of the importance of complex relationships, but they are marginalized to the tasks of information providers for monitoring and adjustment. If Hargreaves had begun with human relationships rather than with the management structures and tasks designed to keep management tidy, then he would have access to the creative energy among professionals. Closed loops may operate in thermostats where corrective control is about bringing 'things' back on track, but not in human interactions. Chaos Theory enables us to understand that you are not necessarily out of control if you are not in control.

Furthermore, there is an obsession with problem-solving within education management products. The effective manager is provided with a series of stages, tasks and systems in order to be able to work through people to get the job done. Problem-solving is aided by controlling problem development by having a consensus value system, collective goals and a sense of purpose combined with collegiate team structures. This is an illusion, but it is being packaged (and repackaged) and sold to educational professionals under the guise of a right to manage. We cannot solve problems, rather it is the issues from which the problems are created that require investigation. Redefining a problem as an opportunity does not help, and in fact is mischievous. If I'm cold then I can switch on the heating, and if I am too warm then I can turn it off. Problem solved? The problem (feeling hot or cold) is seen as being linear, with cause and effect close together, and I am in control of the barrier that I have created. However, the technical action of flicking a switch and obtaining instant relief from cold or heat does not really solve the problem. I have been cold/hot in the past, and no doubt I will be cold/hot again in the future. The barrier that I have created has been there and will continue as long as I am a sentient being (though being cold/hot in my grave still means that the issue is there, but not a live one!). Furthermore, I may make choices independent of feeling hot or cold. I may decide to tolerate the cold in order not to have a large heating bill, or go for a walk to keep warm, and so on. In other words we create, we inherit, we define and we redefine problems. We can put in place short-term measures to deal with manifestations of the problem but we cannot 'clear it up' or 'settle it' or 'close the book'. We can never truly zero base. When the legal system completes a murder case the victim may be buried and the perpetrator in jail but the problem of that and other murders has not been resolved. Problems within social processes are non-linear, cause and effect are distant, and history helps to shape the present. Therefore for educational professionals the key concern is how tasks, processes and events are or are not conceptualized as a problem, and a problem which they as educationalists have to solve. Saul (1992, p.7) has argued that 'a civilisation unable to differentiate between illusion and reality is usually believed to be at the tail end of its existence', and this has messages for the Education Management Industry in its construction of problem-solving imperatives and knowledge. In order to apply in this context, I will take the liberty of paraphrasing Saul (1992) and say that within the Education Management Industry reality is dominated by elites who have spent much of the last decade organizing teachers 'around answers and around structures designed to produce answers' (p.8). In this sense, elites are those who have power positions based on what is promoted as 'expertise' in the form of books, videos, software and inset courses. Management knowledge is controlled through these products: it is targeted, audience specific and exclusive to the management elite within a school. The language of accountability, performance indicators, consensus and quality gives legitimacy. This is an illusion and a dangerous one at that. As Saul (1992) states:

> Thus, among the illusions which have invested our civilization is an absolute belief that the solution to our problems must be a more determined application of rationally organized expertise. The reality is that our problems are largely the product of that application. The illusion is that we have created the most sophisticated society in the history of man. The reality is that the division of knowledge into feudal fiefdoms of expertise has made general understanding and coordinated action not simply impossible but despised and distrusted. (p.8)

What is particularly 'despised and distrusted' within education management products is the concept of professionalism. Traditionally, teachers have focused on professional issues to do with learning, assessment, standards, teaching style, subject context and concepts. Teachers recognized the importance of 'general understanding' of these issues and how structural factors such as the economy had an impact, and also promoted 'coordinated action' in the form of working with parents, and ultimately taking action if the issue was conceptualized as a problem that could undermine learning. Education professionals are told that they now have management problems to do with outcomes, accountability, improvement and change. The issues are not new to educational professionals, and if we strip away the managerialist jargon then we may be able to gain access to understanding that teachers have always been interested in outcomes, but not the ones which are measured in league tables. Teachers have always had a sense of accountability, but they question the current emphasis on leaving a paper trail of proformas and policy documents to prove that they are. Teachers have always been in favour of continuous improvement, but this has been invisible as much creative flair happens outside normal pupil-contact hours, and is not recognized by externally imposed criteria. Teachers have always driven change in teaching and learning styles, examination courses, new materials and technology. However, it has not always been welcomed by the tabloid media and the New Right, who have a different agenda.

Therefore, if educational professionals have failed at all, it has been in how educational and non-educational issues have been conceptualized as problems which they have to solve. Decentralization of the responsibility for educational issues to schools as a result of legislation such as the 1988 Education Reform Act has meant that the management model has been attractive. If schools not only *can* make a difference (teachers have never denied this) but also *have to* make a difference, then schools will take on the structural economic and social problems around them. Equal opportunity policies are important for educational institutions, but they will not manage away the structural injustices in society. Furthermore, 'management by ringbinder' will not provide the real authority to discharge those responsibilities when power over priorities and resources lies with government agencies. Perhaps what we need are management development courses and books which enable professionals to say: we understand that this is an important issue, and we would like to contribute to debate but it is not only our problem. I can expel a child for drug-pushing in the school playground but the school is not the cause of the drugs problem; I can make a member of staff redundant but it does not resolve the underresourcing of education and the structural weaknesses of the economy.

Educational professionals have not been quiet over many of these issues, and OFSTED report after report shows, for example, that schools have refused to solve the legislated problems surrounding collective worship and daily assemblies because it goes against professional judgement and equity. Nevertheless, it does not prevent education management products from continuing to peddle their quick fixes and patent medicines as cure-alls. It seems that professionals are able to live with the sentence in their OFSTED report which says they are not obeying the law. How long can such resistance last when new teachers are entering the profession trained in accordance with minimalist competences?

This needs to be put within a 'bigger picture', and we could trace the development of the Education Management Industry to the worldwide dissatisfaction with education that has led to restructuring in the form of the self-managing school and college (Lawton, 1992; Gordon and Pearce, 1993) and the growth of technical and measurable management competences. In proactively responding to the perceived need to do something, education management has been deluded into thinking it could problem-solve for practitioners. As Sungaila (1990b) has shown:

> Irrespective of how educational administrators are trained, and educational systems are structured and managed, public dissatisfaction will continue to manifest itself in one form or another. Such is the nature of educational reality. (p.4)

Sungaila goes on to argue that those involved in professional development need not keep rushing to develop new courses, books and other product development as a means of demonstrating that they are worthy of existing either structurally or economically. In other words, education management cannot deal with parent, pupil and politician dissatisfaction with schools by collaborating with managerial agendas and making systemic reforms work. Schools will always be a complex issue as their existence and form are a matter for values, ethics, politics and interests. Conceptualizing a school as a small business based on entrepreneurial techniques will not manage these issues away. If educational professionals are unable to resist then we will have educational practitioners who are pragmatic problem-solvers rather than professionals who have a moral and ethical involvement in social issues, and are capable of being pragmatic but are also theorists and thinkers. Education management can only have a role to play for the practitioner if it looks at its role within, and contribution to, knowledge creation, and how it facilitates the practitioner's access to it. As Wheatley (1994) has stated:

> In our past explorations, the tradition was to discover something and then formulate it into answers and solutions that could be widely transferred. But now we are on a journey of mutual and simultaneous exploration. In my view, all we can expect from one another is new and interesting information. We can *not* expect answers. Solutions, as quantum reality teaches, are a temporary event, specific to a context, developed through the relationship of persons and circumstances. There will be no more patrons, waiting expectantly for our return, just more and more explorers venturing out on their own. (pp.150–1)

Chaos Theory enables us to conceptualize education as a complex *human* system in which a full interplay of regenerative forces can take place. The implications of Chaos Theory lie in a debate about what the successful professional behaviours for teachers are. This is not an easy process and as we have seen it requires an engagement with fundamental issues to do with knowledge. For Wheatley (1994), the personal story of developing a new understanding of the universe unfolds throughout her book, and she states:

> the time I formerly spent on detailed planning and analysis I now use to look at the structures that might facilitate relationships. I have come to expect that something useful occurs if I link up people, units, or tasks, even though I cannot determine precise outcomes. And last, I realize more and more that the universe will not cooperate with my desires for determinism. (pp.43–4)

Action–thinking–action is real empowerment because it is based on 'decentralising the location of (and the authority for) knowledge creation' (Winter, 1991, p.474). People do not just respond to the environment, they create it, and therefore what schools and colleges offer to current and potential customers is not about meeting customer needs but about shaping them. This is a new role for managers in being interventionist within the environment by seeing how small changes can have a considerable impact over time as 'creative strategies emerge from instability in a seemingly unintended, uncoordinated manner' (Stacey, 1992, p.20). The investment of time and energy in such dissipative structures is high, but turbulence does not interrupt or interfere – as Sawada and Caley argue, it 'embodies information' (1985, p.16). Hence the use of information and decision-making is by the use of analogy and intuition rather than analysing cause and effect through modelling and statistical forecasting. Wheatley (1994, p.117) acknowledges that 'new knowledge' is from relationships and networks, and goes on to argue that thinking skills or 'intellectual capital' is an essential resource for all workers. Visioning is not about knowledge creation, understanding or dissemination. Visioning is a delusion; its only function is to provide comfort for those uneasy about living with turbulent change. When people find themselves in new situations they learn while doing it and using previous activities to develop meaning and new strategies for creating the future (Stacey, 1992). Therefore effectiveness is not just about measuring up to external and imposed criteria, but about professional judgement and professional standards.

The challenge for the Education Management Industry is to learn that contradiction and conflict are very creative, and that people within an organization will not learn if they are subject to the control of a strong value system, but they will learn if they know how to recognize disorder. It will be difficult to break out of the evangelical myth of the consensus and stability models, but effective management is about being a 'bureaucracy buster' (Dumaine, 1991; Semler, 1989) and 'equilibrium buster' (Jantsch in Wheatley, 1994). Organizations have traditionally recruited and rewarded on the basis of the formal skills which the organization defines as being valid and worthy of the title 'skill'. The butterfly effect allows us to recognize that one person can have an impact and therefore the lesson for teachers is to tap into and encourage the whole skills base of colleagues. When instability disrupts existing patterns of behaviour, organizations can be left bereft of what to do as the old skills are redundant and the training courses for the new ones have not been designed. This is directly linked to equality of opportunity and access, as Gaskell (1992) has shown:

> Women have not had the power to insist that their skills be recognized and valued in the work-place. Their lack of ability to define the work as skilled is not simply a matter of cognition, but is the result of a social process that has had institutional consequences in relation to educational qualifications and opportunities for vocational training, as well as in relation to wages. (p.113)

Therefore real equality of opportunity within educational organizations is about giving recognition to the skills and capacities which staff have as a result of the plurality of their lives.

When events or crises hit individuals and groups there is a spontaneous capacity to organize and respond. Groups form which are fluid and can network with each other while the issue is salient. Many pressure groups have been formed in this way: women at Greenham Common; various groups against the poll tax; miners' wives during the miners' strike of 1984–85. A recent example is the Friends of John McCarthy, for which Jill Morrell describes how:

> Nick [Toksvig] and I felt that we had to act; to go out to the Middle East and see what was happening for ourselves, to talk to people ... All our friends, and especially our colleagues at WTN, were enthusiastic and eager to help. When the management told Nick and me that we couldn't, as planned, go over Christmas and New Year because of staffing problems, colleagues switched their holidays around to make the trip possible. When we realized we would need to organize a small fund-raising evening to pay our way we found ourselves bombarded with help from all sides. It was as if John's friends had been waiting a long, long time to be able to help in some way ... (McCarthy and Morrell, 1993, pp.113–15)

These people showed the capacity for self-organization in which current behaviour patterns are shattered by 'the spontaneous formation of interest groups and coalitions around specific issues, communication about those issues, cooperation and the formation of consensus on and commitment to a response to those issues' (Stacey, 1993, p.242).

Self-organization can be in many forms. It can happen within a bureaucracy like the Friends of John McCarthy and the anti-live animal export protest groups; or it can overthrow a bureaucracy, like Solidarity in Poland. Such social interactions are based on collaboration rather than collusion: there is emphasis on open communication, active listening, a recognition of the learning opportunities. There is the capacity for the individual to be self-motivated, self-regulated and to value the self in order to facilitate action rather than be steered from a distance by policy structures and agencies. This is what Stacey (1993) calls 'communities of practice' where

> People performing closely similar tasks always form informal social groups in which they discuss what they are doing and the environment they are doing it in. They gossip, repeat anecdotes, and tell war stories. They recount the difficulties they have experienced in carrying out particular tasks and others compare these with similar experiences they have had. What is going on when this happens is, however, far more important than pleasant social exchange. What is going on is in fact a vitally important form of learning. (pp.348–9)

Therefore individuals are motivated by intrinsic rewards such as a sense of achievement and feelings of self-worth rather than by extrinsic rewards such as pay and promotion.

Organizations can utilize this energy and commitment in a creative way, enabling political activity to take place, rather than trying to overlay it or eradicate it by formal structures. Political action in the forming of coalitions around key issues and building power blocs is the source of innovation and creativity. Micro-politics in educational institutions has been documented (Ball, 1987), and more recently Ganderton (1991) has identified the important role of the 'subversive' within the organization. The subversive is in contrast to the 'conformist' and 'isolate' and is defined as someone who through their attitude and viewpoints is seen to be 'at variance with the prevailing organizational view.' (p.32). However, as Ganderton argues, both theory and management training identify the role of the subversive as that of a saboteur and therefore:

> Management strategies have sought to marginalise/neutralise such people because they are assumed to be of only negative value. (p.36)

However, Chaos Theory allows us to see the subversive or the maverick in a positive way as an enabler and emancipator. Hence the capacity for individual and group learning is great; Morrell (McCarthy and Morrell, 1993) has shown the impact of the Friends of John McCarthy at critical points in creating rather than visioning the future:

> The Friends' campaign achieved its objective, to make the hostages an issue in Britain; a political problem that would have to be resolved before the resumption of any meaningful relationship with Iran. (p.495)

Spontaneous self-organizing groups cannot be controlled by managers, as membership is self-participating, self-empowering, self-regulating and self-destructing (Stacey, 1993). Behaviour is not random but based on 'self reference' (Jantsch, 1980, p.26), i.e. disorder and turbulence generate information for change, but change is within an environmental context. As Wheatley (1994) states,

> As it changes, it does so by referring to itself; whatever future form it takes will be consistent with its already established identity ... [Changes] always are consistent with what has gone on before, with the history and identity of the system. (p.94)

This is nowhere better illustrated than by contrasting self-organization with self-managing teams, as illustrated in Table 5.1. The main message from the comparison outlined in the table is that managers cannot install effective management systems but can intervene in the energetic and creative human interactions already happening around them. Therefore management training and development based on strategies, tools and rational cycles for proactively empowering people is an expensive illusion. Leadership is a product of human networks within a context rather than a product of role hierarchy and contrived cultural norms. Furthermore, we cannot have a meaningful debate about the quality of teaching and learning, and how to raise levels of achievement for all children unless teachers take control rather than wait to be given it. This is where the potential for real school improvement is located. The growth of the expert manager in education not only denies teacher professionalism by elevating managerial knowledge and skills, but is also cutting off the professional from information analysis and interpretation. As Wheatley (1994) has stated:

> We often limit their potential because we circumscribe them with rules and chains of command or give them narrow mandates or restrict their access to information. But if we liberate them from those confines and allow them greater autonomy, constrained more by purpose than by rules or preset expectations, then their potential for generating information is great. (p.115)

Table 5.1. Comparing self-managing teams and self-organization networks

Self-managing teams	Self-organization networks
Are formally installed with clear terms of reference and a reporting imperative. Therefore legitimacy is organizationally defined. Can be temporary or permanent.	Informal temporary groups form spontaneously around issues. Legitimacy derived from the issue and can be in line with the formal organization or in conflict with it.
Are controlled through rules on how to operate by managers who have installed the team(s). Teams are proactively created often using team roles; e.g. Belbin to facilitate the process.	Cannot be controlled directly. Managers like anyone else can intervene to influence the boundaries. Group participants decide on who takes part and what the boundaries are. There are no predetermined roles and no leaders until they develop through social and political interaction.
Are intended to increase participation by flattening the traditional hierarchical structure.	Networks operate in conflict with and are constrained by the hierarchical structure.
Delegation of power to proactively created teams is supposed to lead to consensus. Norms are predetermined and ensure equilibrium: first, strategy and decision making are controlled by the vision and mission of the school/college; and second, the team process is controlled by INSET based on the linear model of forming, storming, norming, and performing.	Power is unequal and energizes the networks through conflict and also operates as a constraint. Control is through the political and social interactions, and norms emerge from this. This is destabilizing in that the networks are sometimes in line with the formal structure and sometimes in competition with it.
The hierarchy empowers the teams.	People empower themselves.

Source: Derived from Stacey, 1993, p.243.

The challenge for continuous professional development is in enabling teachers to understand the context in which they exercise their professional skills and knowledge. Perhaps it is time that teachers engaged in professing what is central to being a professional. Chaos Theory provides opportunities to explore how learning is about sharing and changing perceptions through group interaction which discovers, questions, makes critical choices and takes action. Effective organizations are more about resiliency than stability.

CHAPTER 6

Heresy

The field of education management has a number of interesting issues to debate and discuss, and this book has been about conceptualizing issues around the question: what is education management for? This goes beyond the definitions of 'application' and 'practitioner orientation' to consider some fundamental issues. It is somewhat heretical not to debate whether education management is efficient, effective and economic, but to question whether it should be. I am using the term 'heretic' in the way characterized by Hargreaves (1994):

> if missions develop loyalty among the faithful and confidence among the committed, they also create heresy among those who question, differ and doubt. The narrow and more fervent the mission, the greater and more wide-spread the heresy. For the missionary, heresies are beyond the walls of wisdom, the boundaries of belief. (p.163)

The Education Management Industry has a mission to inform the practitioner of the management problems he or she has or will have and to promote management models as solutions. The heresy that I am speaking is both *substantive* in that I am questioning the Education Management Industry's promotion of visioning, but it is also *generic* in that I am also asking why it is promoting visioning (Hargreaves, 1994, p.164).

The Jurassic Management metaphor has facilitated an understanding of the Education Management Industry as one which promotes a form of organizational control through:

- creating a vision of the future;
- a leader articulating that vision;
- a leader using the vision to drive for change;
- building commitment to the vision by a shared culture and consensus;
- using the vision to determine the long-term planning and resource management priorities and choices;
- living the vision in day-to-day behaviour and activities;

- marketing the vision outside the organization.

We might therefore argue that if schools are better managed and more effective, then the Education Management Industry is achieving its purpose, and hence has legitimacy. If we have league tables to show that attendance is being better managed and OFSTED reports which show that a school is good value for money, then the operationalization of management techniques and processes is vindicated. However, there are deeper issues about connecting the purpose of the Education Management Industry with the policy context and the drive for managerialism within the public sector. The unreflexive acceptance and promotion of the management imperative by the Education Management Industry provides an alternative view in which 'management by ringbinder' is about product development in order to guarantee job creation through consultancy and publications. As long as the management imperative is 'sold' as the solution to constructed 'educational problems' then we have to debate the purpose of education management as a part of a restructuring of the public sector in which:

- management must act, perform, make it happen and have a right to manage disconnected from the social and economic context;
- management is separate in language, form, and function to teaching;
- education has been defined according to economic indicators, and therefore social development and innovation are connected with efficiency and effectiveness rather than equity, justice and liberty;
- efficiency and effectiveness of learning is directly linked with the innovation and application of technology (databases, spreadsheets, e-mail, etc.) in relation to information gathering and dissemination;
- teachers have to be controlled through management techniques by teams, vision and mission, and corporate collaboration.

Therefore the purpose of 'management by ringbinder' is to eclipse the professional role of the teacher rather than to develop it. *Jurassic Park* (Crichton, 1991) shows that this management ideology is giving permission to managers in educational institutions to feel happy with a different way of controlling the organization compared to traditional and discredited bureaucratic methods.

Recent legislation and policy changes have decentralized the responsibility for the performance of externally defined tasks, but has not decentralized knowledge creation. The Education Management Industry sees its role as helping the reflective practitioner to understand how to perform these tasks by getting it right. Teachers are therefore consumers of management knowledge and techniques in which they are encouraged to exercise their Belbin (1981, 1993) roles while undertaking a SWOT analysis. This creates the illusion of teacher-control of their work, when in effect control lies with those who initiate and 'manage' these so-called collegiate processes. The teacher is powerless and is therefore neutralized (Davies, 1990, p.17), and this is supported by new technology in which useful knowledge is that which can be processed, quantified and delivered at the right time, to the right person, to make effective and efficient decisions. A teacher asking: who programmed this computer, and what for? is conceptualized as dysfunctional.

Teachers are operating in a contradictory environment which is potentially creative, but they are being simultaneously deskilled and therefore are unable to tap into it. On the one hand, as Hargreaves (1994) as shown, there are enormous implications for teachers' work from living in a post-modern society where 'doubt is pervasive, tradition is in retreat, and moral and scientific certainty have lost their credibility' (p.57). But on the other hand, teachers are vulnerable to modernist left-overs in the form of external improvement and effectiveness strategies in the curriculum and pedagogy (Hargreaves, 1994). This is fertile ground for the Education Management Industry, as in the midst of uncertainty and turbulence it has presented competences, leadership and consensus value systems as a solution. The Education Management Industry has presented a simulated reality in the form of theme park management. As we purchase our education management product we are taken through a *Jurassic Park* experience in which there is a replicated reality far away from reality. We leave with a feeling that things can be better, and this affects our engagement with the alternative. Appignanesi and Garratt (1995) provide us with an alternative in the form of the Holocaust Memorial Museum in Washington, DC, in which you can stroll through evil, watch 'historical snuff movies' and follow the fate of a particular inmate whose ID you adopt for the visit. They conclude that, 'at the end, you'll find visitors' ID cards dumped in litter bins among the pop bottles and chocolate wrappers. Your hyper-reality tour is over' (p.122). Can we as teachers stroll through the structural injustices of the education system as long as we can confirm that we are in a marketplace in which we must do our best on behalf of the children in our care? It was justice, ethics and humanity that closed the concentration camps down, and it is somewhat ironic that on the basis of efficiency and effectiveness they would still be open. The failure of Jurassic Park illustrates that we cannot nor should not create organized human relationships that are based on simplistic notions of interaction and control.

Expertise is no longer institutionally located (in the school, the LEA or the university) but is a commodity to be purchased. Therefore the teacher's job is to buy it in, and this commercial exchange ensures that knowledge, skills and understanding are related to the perceived needs of the teacher as manager. We get what we ask for, and therefore the skill is in defining need rather than knowing ideas. In the general move towards practitioner relevance and the rubbishing of the academic, we have failed to see the creation of a new elite which is more pervasive and dangerous than the ivory tower mentality which we have loved to ridicule. We are all academics and this aspect of our professionalism is currently very unfashionable as we are 'committed to the advancement of learning even (especially) where its use is not immediately evident. The discipline, too is a "client"' (*Higher Education Review*, 1995, p.4). Once the professional is disciplined by competences the networking with ideas is broken. Theory and theorizing is ridiculed, and 'making it happen' has more currency. However, as Inglis (1985) has so forcefully stated:

> ... those who refuse all theory, who speak of themselves as plain, practical people, and virtuous in virtue of having no theory, are in the grip of theories which manacle them and keep them immobile, because they have no way of thinking about them and therefore of taking them off. They aren't theory-free; they are stupid theorists. (p.40)

The growth of experts in the form of consultancies is not a new democracy but another elite. The accountability of consultants is to the market and not their peers. As Saul (1992) has stated, the power of experts is 'not on the effect with which they use that knowledge but on the effectiveness with which they control its use'. This control over knowledge by the Education Management Industry ensures that management as presented in the form of training manuals and/or experiences cannot be open to all teachers. Developing management knowledge is accessed on the basis of funds and therefore must be targeted at where it can achieve value for money, and so is disconnected from pedagogy and educational leadership. Furthermore, by constructing management knowledge without reference to debates in the social sciences, managers are presented with only a partial knowing.

Is it possible or even desirable for teachers to maintain their political beliefs in the 'cultures of uncertainty' as identified by Hargreaves (1994)? For Hargreaves there is an important shift from *'scientific certainty*, the certainty grounded in proven principles of generalized applicability' to *'situated certainty ...* the certainty that teachers and others can collectively glean from their shared practical knowledge of their immediate context and the problems it presents' (p.59). However, in promoting 'situated certainty' based on the 'search for missions, visions and continuous improvement', Hargreaves is enabling the invasion of the human resource management model rather than working with 'resourceful humans' (Bottery, 1992, p.6). Furthermore, while the collapse of the Berlin Wall may symbolize the decline of the single political idea located within an institution like a political party or a state, it does not signal the collapse of political ideas and collectives. The rejection of traditional institutions for channelling political ideas is a rejection of how they have been managed rather than a rejection of what people believe in. The new science of chaos allows us to see that there is validity in the rejection of scientific certainty, but 'situated certainty' is not the new prescription. Rather the development of meaning in the generation of political ideas comes from *self-renewing uncertainty*. The supposed collapse of the meta-narratives of history such as Marxism and capitalism does not mean that teachers (and other public sector workers) should become vulnerable to the new meta-narrative of management.

These issues do relate to the concept and reality of liberal democracy and I will not repeat the excellent examination by Davies (1990) and Bottery (1992) of what this means for education management. However, what is pertinent is that if knowledge creation (both content and process) is owned and controlled by management elites, whether they are knowledge producers in the form of the Education Management Industry or knowledge consumers in the form of senior management teams, then this is profoundly anti-democratic. Teachers become like actors in a TV soap opera in which they act out the drama while the script is written elsewhere. The consequences of this have been eloquently stated in Callahan's (1962) *Cult of Efficiency*:

> The future of our free society requires that our schools be centers of learning and not factories or playgrounds. To make them so will require educators who are students and scholars, not accountants or public relations men. (pp.260–1)

This type of insight is missing within the Education Management Industry. Breaking out of the managerialist and consultancy mind-set of 'how to do it' for prescriptive action is not easy, and there may be occasions within this book when the sediments are still evident in my own thinking and writing. As Sawada and Caley (1985) have argued, there are no guarantees, and after years of 'quick fix' training manuals this statement is a learning process in itself.

Jurassic management: regeneration

In Chapter 1, I presented Extinction Theory as a means of understanding why we need to ask questions about the complex social behaviours which are responsible for the Education Management Industry. How do the books, videos, multimedia packages come to be written and produced? How and why are Master's programmes written and validated? Brochures designed and marketed, and students recruited? Networks of core and part-time staff created and sustained? In approaching these questions we are approaching a reflective and reflexive understanding of the field of education management and the location of the Education Management Industry within it. If we investigated this on the basis of Newtonian physics, then education management would be conceptualized as a 'thing' which can be observed, deconstructed, analysed and put back together. If, however, we live in a quantum world, then the emphasis is on relationships, and it is accepted that 'our acts of observation are part of the process that brings forth the manifestation of what we are observing' (Wheatley, 1994, p.36). Field theory (see Wheatley, 1994, Chapter 3) enables us to look beyond the visible and see that there

> ... are unseen structures, occupying space and becoming known to us through their effects ... Fields encourage us to think of a universe that more closely resembles an ocean, filled with interpenetrating influences and invisible structures that connect. This is a much richer portrait of the universe; in the field world, there are potentials for action everywhere, anywhere two fields meet.
>
> (Wheatley, 1994, pp.49 and 51)

Therefore what is interesting is the 'meeting' or the 'collision' of two fields. This book has charted some of the observable collisions between the participants within the Education Management Industry and other educational analysts. In particular the growth of Education Policy Sociology has provided an interesting challenge; it is identified as being 'rooted in the social science tradition, historically informed and drawing on qualitative and illuminative techiques' (Ozga, 1987). The collision is not a new observation. It is now over fifteen years since Glatter (1979) raised questions about the status of education management and how it related to the work of policy scholars. Glatter argues that the dichotomy between policy as a macro-feature and management as a technical feature is false. He argues his case on a number of grounds: firstly, the conceptual tools used to understand the macro- and micro-levels are the same; and, secondly, in empirical terms the distinction between policy as a value-based study and management as an operational/technique-based study is false, as what goes on in school must have a value base and cannot be separate from educational purpose. Part of Glatter's agenda is not only to show that education management is not the poor relation to policy studies and to try to eliminate perceived snobbery in how the worth of policy studies is judged higher in comparison to management studies, but also to establish a case that management studies have a distinct role to play. The case is put forward that courses in education management should not and are not just narrowly focusing on techniques, nor are they purely academic in the development of knowledge and understanding of the field separate to practice. Rather education management courses should develop *capability* in where the emphasis is on the method of learning in which management development is based on an interaction between experience and research.

Glatter's (1979) use of a 'continuum' is of interest as the collision is not substantive; all those interested in learning are interested in educational issues and in particular in the practical implications of policy and legislative change. It could be that the collision is one of position: does the growth of the Education Management Industry fracture the continuum? It is clear that the industry is disconnected from the importance of history, explanatory theory and 'illuminating' research which is advocated by Education Policy Sociology. The Education Management Industry is concerned with prescriptions for problems, while Education Policy Sociology asks why issues are defined as educational problems, who by and for what purpose? While the Education Management Industry is about promoting management tasks and concepts to the teacher in order to control the professional development agenda, Education Policy Sociology is about investigating and evaluating education policies, and the impact of those policies on the lives and work of teachers and pupils in schools which have made them vulnerable to the management control of professional development. Does this make one field or two? A quantum view of the world suggests that it is more complex than a one-dimensional continuum, and consequently more fascinating for the researcher. Who writes in which journals? Who is invited to lead and speak at which seminars? Who networks through all kinds of media with whom? This is not a 'them and us' issue and if it is turned into a debate about academic snobbery, then we will be stuck along a fractured continuum of: I get my hands dirty by working with real practitioners with real problems while you sit in your office dreaming unrealistic dreams. As Angus (1994) has stated in response to Ozga's (1992) critique of education management publications:

> I cannot stress too strongly that, despite the general dismissal of such texts by sociologists of education, their influence in the arena of educational practice is profound. Social critics need to understand and appreciate that these books address very real problems as experienced by school administrators, their staffs and their school communities. That is why the texts are popular and publishers are happy to produce a stream of them. To the extent that they engage with and offer solutions to what participants perceive to be practical problems, they cannot be dismissed out of hand. Indeed, they are likely to be seen as more relevant to practice than sociological analysis. That is why it is important for people working in the sociology of education to continue to apply their analyses in ways that engage with the day-to-day work of practitioners. Recent work in policy sociology (Ball, 1990; Bowe and Ball, 1992) has been able to take this direction without sacrificing theoretical cogency. (pp.80–1)

Therefore the management of institutions can be improved, but the border-line between having an agenda of options and presenting a prescription is so blurred that it is easy to slip into the latter rather than participate in the debate about the former. This paints an interesting picture of a complex networking of educational professionals, and therefore my statements about heresy are seen in a different light and will be seen in different ways by different observers. If you have doubts about how education management has been and is being described, understood and explained, then does it make me wrong or is it that there are different ways of knowing? I've communicated my observations – why don't you? There is no such thing as the objective truth in social processes, but we can share meaning in the developmental process of the field. Self-organization facilitates collisions and so observable behaviour facilitates challenge and learning.

What does the future hold for the field of education management? If this was a 'management-by-ringbinder' product I could celebrate how far we have come before moving on to provide a strategic tool to control the future. Complementing this I could crystal ball gaze and identify the key issues for education management, for example, what is going to be the impact of information technology such as video conferencing and the Internet on in-service provision and pedagogy? However, what this book has been about is to challenge the Education Management Industry to take a reflective and reflexive approach to the context in which more and more sophisticated product development is taking place. Chaos Theory enables us to understand that we cannot plan the future but rather we create it by the options and critical choices we make now. The market continues to be a relevant option: products have to be sold; managerial paper trails in higher education departments have to be left; and people need to keep their jobs. It would be naive of any observer to suggest otherwise. However, there may be other options which a commitment to the market is limiting recognition of, and it lies with a deeper understanding of the reflective practitioner. Pertinent questions in this area are: do you know what happens when people go on courses, or when they read a book like Caldwell and Spinks (1988)? Do we really know what impact education management products have? This is not market research so that we can find out more insecurities in order to manufacture more prescriptive solutions, but social science research in which we are investigating what is actually happening and what the nature of the partnership is between reflective practitioners. In purchasing and participating in the product (whether reading or attending a course) the teacher becomes a part of the industry as consumer, no matter how limited the engagement. It is this complex relationship and the connection between reflective practitioners both formally inside and outside all sectors of education which is worthy of investigation.

Maguire and Ball (1994) have noted that practitioner work is rarely published, and is usually located on university bookshelves where it remains unread. How and why do teachers in schools come to publish their research? Why are there practitioners who may have something to say but do not publish? How does a practitioner come to know and understand what is worthy of publication? Why are there practitioners who have been involved in the development of management strategies who are written out of the story by the prescriptive nature of the ringbinder? This is tied up with issues to do with status, power and staking a claim for recognition. We might therefore ask questions about how and why teachers in schools become lecturers in higher education. Why do headteachers retire and become OFSTED inspectors and consultants? In other words, what is worthy of investigation is how the Education Management Industry investigates its claims to the authority and legitimacy of what it is doing. This has to be more than the importance of 'I am or have been until recently working at the management face and therefore I know and understand what it is like'. It is an essential part of the glue which holds the networks together, but 'expertise' is constructed, and as Winter (1991) has argued, sociology has a role to investigate 'the cultural stratifications implicit in the structures of "expertise"' (p.479). In this way we have the option to consider the development of management expertise and what it means for our understanding of what we are doing and why we are doing it. As we continue to live and work in restructured, leaner, flatter matrices, we can consider whether we are promoting the practitioner as the prisoner of the management project which has been so central to education policy and legislation. By networking within the social sciences then knowledge production within the Education Management Industry can be seen in a different way. As Winter (1991) has argued:

> ... 'knowledge' is not conceived as an achievement of representative accuracy, but as a practice of critical and developmental engagement on the part of citizens in general with the experience of their social responsibilities. (p.479)

The decentralization of knowledge creation for the reflective practitioner is strong within the social sciences literature (Smyth, 1992; Winter, 1991) and provides the potential for the teacher, lecturer, professor, consultant and inspector to connect with some interesting debates and issues which are directly relevant to theory and practice. Debate about managerialism within and about the public sector is not about turning the clock back, but is about looking at what the current issues are and the role of the educational professional within them.

Thinking globally, acting locally

In raising the issue of the development of the Education Management Industry within a publication I am presenting an agenda which is fundamental to my ongoing research project but is not exclusive to me. We are all a part of this industry and therefore we are a part of the debate about it, otherwise we will be both participants and victims of the managerial oppression it promotes. I would like to encourage a rich and vibrant debate within the complexity of current and potential relationships. In supporting this I would like to use the 'procedural points' suggested by Winter (1991, pp.477-9) as 'indications' for investigation in order to develop the research work of myself as a reflective practitioner:

- Theories: Winter wishes to 'take theories as *metaphors*, i.e. representations of other experiences which are available as *possible resources* for the *re-interpretation* of experience.' My ongoing research is concerned with looking at the relevance of Foucault (1972) and knowledge creation; Bourdieu's concepts of Field and Habitus (Jenkins, 1992); Gramsci's (1971) hegemony in understanding the growth and development of the field of education management.
- Dialectics: for Winter, the tension between theory and practice can be explored by 'seeking contradictions, seeking unity underlying apparent difference, seeking difference within apparent

unity, placing apparently isolated events within a social and historical context'. My research is concerned with locating the development of education management within the policy context, and what the management imperative is about and who has a stake within it and why.

- Collaboration: Winter argues that 'the relationships of inquiry need to be collaborative and, hence, mutually developmental for all those involved', and within my research project I am working with colleagues within the field of education management on their narrative biographies concerned with professional choices and position.

- Reflexive Awareness: Winter argues that the 'guidelines for contesting authoritative interpretive judgements are provided by the process of reflexive critique', and therefore my research has within it a research biography in which there are the opportunities to present the unfolding research process, discuss ethical choices and to critically interrogate judgements.

- Writing: Winter advocates the use of 'developmental writing' and in particular it is 'the reformulation of one's interpretive resources, and is, therefore, both personal and collaborative: reading provides resources; a library is a source of collaborators'. Therefore the process of researching the history of education management is being done with, rather than to, field participants.

- Dissemination: Winter argues that 'if practitioners' reflective work is to be a basis for the general development of collective understanding, new and more decentralised forms of publication will be needed ...' and therefore I will not only publish in books and journals, but interact further in the complexity of social relationships – expect a call, a visit or an Internet page. A simple question: why did BEAS (British Educational Administration Society) become BEMAS with the word Management inserted? I find this fascinating and would welcome more information: When did it happen? Who wanted the change and why? Were you involved? Did it matter to you then? Does it still matter?

Chaos Theory recognizes the importance of interaction, networking and political activity in which there is a climate of open debate, and the capacity for people to self-organize, to be self-motivating and to be tolerant. I would finally like to return to the invitation I gave in the Preface and to take the challenge a stage further by asking you to participate in debating with me: what is the Education Management Industry for and what is legitimizing it? The Education Management Industry cannot go on peddling its products on change management without a review of how it itself has grown within the changing field of education management. As Gleick (1987) has noted, Chaos theorists faced 'incomprehension, resistance, anger, acceptance' (p.304), so hang on, it's going to be a bumpy ride within the education management theme park.

Postscript: invitation

You are cordially invited to contact me and to participate in this ongoing research. Your account of your professional life history, the choices you have made, the nature of your work within your past and current professional portfolio and your views on the development of the field of education management are all of interest and central to our collective concerns.

Bibliography

Acker, J. and Van Houten, D.R. (1992) Differential recruitment and control: the sex structuring of organizations. In Mills, A.J. and Tancred, P. *Gendering Organizational Analysis*. London: Sage.

Adams, N. (1993) *Legal Issues and the Self-managing School*. Harlow: Longman.

Adler, S., Laney, J. and Packer, M. (1993) *Managing Women*. Buckingham: Open University Press.

Al-Khalifa, E. (1986) Can education management learn from industry? In Hoyle, E. and McMahon, A. *World Yearbook of Education 1986: The Management of Schools*. London: Kogan Page.

Anderson, G.L. and Dixon, A. (1993) Paradigm shifts and site-based management in the United States: toward a paradigm of social empowerment. In Smyth, J. (ed.) *A Socially Critical View of the Self-managing School*. London: Falmer Press.

Angus, L. (1993) Democratic participation or efficient site management: the social and political location of the self-managing school. In Smyth, J. (ed.) *A Socially Critical View of the Self-Managing School*. London: Falmer Press.

Angus, L. (1994) Sociological analysis and education management: the social context of the self-managing school. *British Journal of Sociology of Education* **15** (1), 79–91.

Appignanesi, R. and Garratt, C. with Sardar, Z. and Curry, P. (1995) *Postmodernism for Beginners*. Cambridge: Icon Books Ltd.

Apple, M.W. (1989) Critical introduction: ideology and the state in education policy. In Dale, R. *The State and Education Policy*. Buckingham: Open University Press.

Audit Commission (1993) *Adding up the Sums: Schools Management of Their Finances*. London: HMSO.

Aylett, J. (1991) *Managing a New Era: An Educational Management Training Pack*. London: Hodder and Stoughton.

Back, K., Back, K. and Bates, T. (1991) *Assertiveness at Work* (second edition). Maidenhead: McGraw Hill Book Company.

Ball, S.J. (1987) *The Micropolitics of the School*. London: Routledge.

Ball, S.J. (1990a) *Politics and Policymaking in Education: Explorations in Policy Sociology*. London: Routledge.

Ball, S.J. (1990b) Management as moral technology: a Luddite analysis. In Ball, S.J.(ed.) *Foucault and Education*. London: Routledge.

Ball, S. J. (1990c) Self-doubt and soft-data: social and technical trajectories in ethnographic fieldwork. *Qualitative Studies in Education* **3** (2), 157–71.

Ball, S.J. (1993) Culture, cost and control: self-management and entrepreneurial schooling in England and Wales. In Smyth, J. (ed.) *A Socially Critical View of the Self-Managing School*. London: Falmer.

Ball, S.J. (1994) Some reflections on policy theory: a brief response to Hatcher and Troyna. *Journal of Education Policy* **9** (2), 171–82.

Barber, M., Evans, A. and Johnson, M. (1995) *An Evaluation of the National Scheme of School Teacher Appraisal*. London: HMSO.

Barker, B. (1991) *The Cambridgeshire Management Workshops: Professional Development and Practical Guidance for School Life in the 1990s*. Dereham: Peter Francis Publishers.

Baron, G. and Taylor, W. (1969) *Educational Administration and the Social Sciences*. London: The Athlone Press.

Belbin, R.M. (1981) *Management Teams: Why They Succeed or Fail*. Oxford: Butterworth-Heinemann Ltd.

Belbin, R.M. (1993) *Team Roles at Work*. Oxford: Butterworth-Heinemann Ltd.

Bell, J. (1987) *Doing Your Research Project*. Milton Keynes: Open University Press.

Bell, L. (1989) Ambiguity models and secondary schools: a case study. In Bush, T. (ed.) *Managing Education: Theory and Practice*. Buckingham: Open University Press.

Bell, L. (1991) Educational management: an agenda for the 1990s. *Educational Management and Administration* **19** (3), 136–40.

Bell, L. (1992) *Managing Teams in Secondary Schools*. London: Routledge.

Bennett, H. with Lister, M. and McManus, M. (1992) *Teacher Appraisal: Survival and Beyond*. Harlow: Longman.

Blanchard, K. and Johnson, S (1983) *The One Minute Manager*. London: Fontana.

Blanchard, K., Oncken, W. and Burrows, H. (1989) *The One Minute Manager Meets the Monkey*. London: Fontana Collins.

Blanchard, T., Lovell, B. and Ville, N. (1989) *Managing Finance in Schools*. London: Cassell.

Bollington, R. and Bradley, H. (1991) *Training for Appraisal: A Set of Distance Learning Materials*. Cambridge: Cambridge Institute of Education.

Bone, T.R. (1982) Educational administration. *British Journal of Educational Studies* **30** (1), February, pp.32–42.

Bottery, M. (1992) *The Ethics of Educational Management*. London: Cassell.

Bottery, M. (1994) *Lessons for Schools? A Comparison of Business and Educational Management*. London: Cassell.

Bowe, R. and Ball, S. with Gold, A. (1992) *Reforming Education and Changing Schools*. London: Routledge.

Bush, T. (1989) School management structures – theory and practice. *Educational Management and Administration* **17**, 3–8.

Bush, T. (1995) *Theories of Educational Management* (second edition). London: Paul Chapman Publishing Limited.

Busher, H. and Saran, R. (eds) (1995) *Managing Teachers as Professionals in Schools*. London: Kogan Page.

Busher, H. and Saran, R. (1995) Managing staff professionally. In Busher, H. and Saran, R. (eds) (1995) *Managing Teachers as Professionals in Schools*. London: Kogan Page.

Caldwell, B.J. and Spinks, J.M. (1988) *The Self-managing School*. Lewes: Falmer Press.

Caldwell, B.J. and Spinks, J.M. (1992) *Leading the Self-managing School*. London: Falmer Press.

Callahan, R.E. (1962) *Education and the Cult of Efficiency*. Chicago: University of Chicago Press.

Clarke, J., Cochrane, A. and McLaughlin, E. (eds) (1994) *Managing Social Policy*. London: Sage.

Clarke, M. and Stewart, J. (1992) Empowerment: a theme for the 1990s. *Local Government Studies* **18** (2), 18–26.

Codd, J.A. (1993) Managerialism, market liberalism and the move to self-managing schools in New Zealand. In Smyth, J. (ed.) *A Socially Critical View of the Self-managing School*. London: Falmer Press.

Cohen, L. and Mannion, L. (1980) *Research Methods in Education* (3rd edn). London: Routledge and Kegan Paul.

Cohen, M.D. and March, J.G. (1989) Leadership and ambiguity. In Bush, T. *Managing Education: Theory and Practice*. Buckingham: Open University Press.

Cooke, D.H., Hamon, R.H. and Proctor, A.M. (1938) *Principles of School Administration*. Minneapolis.

Cox, R.W. (1981) Social forces, states, and world order: beyond international relations theory. *Millennium* **10** (2), 126–55.

Craig, I. (1987) *Primary School Management in Action*. Harlow: Longman.

Craig, I. (1989) *Primary Headship in the 1990s*. Harlow: Longman.

Crawford, M., Kydd, L. and Parker, S. (1994) *Educational Management in Action*. London: Paul Chapman.

Crichton, M. (1991) *Jurassic Park*. London: Arrow.

Crichton, M. (1995) *The Lost World*. London: Century.

Curtis, R.K. (1990) Complexity and predictability: the application of chaos theory to economic forecasting. *Futures Research Quarterly* Winter, 57–70.

Cziko, G.A. (1989) Unpredictability and indeterminism in human behavior: arguments and implications for educational research. *Educational Researcher* April, 17–25.

Dale, R. (1989) *The State and Education Policy*. Milton Keynes: Open University Press.

Dale, R. (1990) The Thatcherite project in education: the case of the City Technology Colleges. *Journal of Critical Social Policy* **9** (3), 4–19.

Davies, B. and Ellison, L. (1990) *Managing the Primary School Budget*. Plymouth: Northcote House Publishers Ltd.

Davies, B. and Ellison, L. (1991) *Marketing the Secondary School*. Harlow: Longman.

Davies, B. and Ellison, L. (1992) *School Development Planning*. Harlow: Longman.

Davies, B. and Ellison, L. (eds) (1994) *Managing the Effective Primary School*. Harlow: Longman.

Davies, B., Ellison, L., Osborne, A. and West-Burnham, J. (1990) *Education Management for the 1990s*. Harlow: Longman.

Davies, L. (1990) *Equity and Efficiency? School Management in an International Context*. Lewes: Falmer.

Davies, M. (1992) The little boy said ... 'The emperor still isn't wearing any clothes'. *The Curriculum Journal* **3** (1), 3–10.

Davies, J.L. and Morgan, A.W. (1983) Management of higher education in a period of contraction and uncertainty. In Body-Barratt, O., Bush, T., Goodey, J., McNay, J. and Preedy, M. (eds) *Approaches to Post School Management*. London: Harper and Row.

de Bono, E. (1993) *Surpetition: Going Beyond Competition*. London: Harper/Collins.

Demaine, J. (1993) The New Right and the self-managing school. In Smyth, J. (ed.) *A Socially Critical View of the Self-managing School*. London: Falmer Press.

DES (1985) *Better Schools*. London: HMSO.

DES (1991) *The Education (School Teacher Appraisal) Regulations* No. 1511. London: HMSO.

DFE (1994) *Education Means Business*. London: HMSO.

Downie, R.S. (1990) Professions and professionalism. *Journal of Philosophy of Education* **24** (2), 147–59.

Dumaine, B. (1991) The bureaucracy busters. *Fortune*, June 17, 26–36.

Edelman, M. (1964) *The Symbolic Uses of Politics*. Urbana: University of Illinois Press.

Edelman, M. (1977) *Political Language: Words That Succeed and Policies That Fail*. New York: Academic Press.

Elliott, G. and Hall, V. (1994) FE Inc. – business orientation in further education and the introduction of human resource management. *School Organisation* **14** (1), 3–10.

Elliott, J. (1991) *Action Research for Educational Change*. Buckingham: Open University Press.

Ellison, L. (1990a) Managing stress in schools. In Davies, B., Ellison, L., Osborne, A. and West-Burnham, J. (1990) *Education Management for the 1990s*. Harlow: Longman.

Ellison, L. (1990b) Effective time management. In Davies, B., Ellison, L., Osborne, A. and West-Burnham, J. (1990) *Education Management for the 1990s*. Harlow: Longman.

Ellison, L. (1994) The current educational context. In Davies, B. and Ellison, L. (eds) (1994) *Managing the Effective Primary School*. Harlow: Longman.

Everard, B. (1995) Values as central to competent professional practice. In Busher, H. and Saran, R. (eds) *Managing Teachers as Professionals in Schools*. London: Kogan Page.

Farnham, D. and Horton, S. (eds.) (1992a) *Managing the New Public Services*. Basingstoke: Macmillan Press Ltd.

Farnham, D. and Horton, S. (1992b) Human resources management in the new public sector: leading or following private employer practice. *Public Policy and Administration* **7** (3), Winter, 42–55.

Fayol, H. (1916) *Administration industrielle et generale*. Translated by Storrs, C. (1949) as *General and Industrial Management* London: Pitman.

Feintuck, M. (1994) *Accountability and Choice in Schooling*. Buckingham: Open University Press.

Fergusson, R. (1994) Managerialism in education. In Clarke, J., Cochrane, A. and McLaughlin, E. (1994) *Managing Social Policy*. London: Sage.

Ferchat, R.A. (1990) The chaos factor. *The Corporate Board* May/June, 8–12.

Fisher, R. and Ury, W. (1991) *Getting to Yes* (second edition). London: Business Books Limited.

Foucault, M. (1972) *The Archaeology of Knowledge*. London: Tavistock Publications.

Fullan, M.G. with Steigelbauer, S. (1991) *The New Meaning of Educational Change*. London: Cassell.

Ganderton, P.S. (1991) Subversion and the organization: some theoretical considerations. *Educational Management and Administration* **19** (1), 30–6.

Gaskell, J. (1992) *Gender Matters from School to Work*. Buckingham: Open University Press.

Gelsthorpe, L. (1992) Response to Martyn Hammersley's paper 'On feminist methodology'. *Sociology* **26** (2), 213–18.

Gewirtz, S., Ball, S.J. and Bowe, R. (1993) Values and ethics in the education marketplace: the case of Northwark Park. *International Studies in Sociology of Education* **3** (2), 233–54.

Gillborn, D. (1994) The micro-politics of macro reform. *British Journal of Sociology of Education* **15** (2), 147–64.

Gillen, T. (1992) *Assertiveness for Managers*. Aldershot: Gower.

Glatter, R. (1972) *Management Development for the Education Profession*. London: Harrap.

Glatter, R. (1979) Educational 'policy' and 'management': one field or two? In Bush, T., Glatter, R., Goodey, J. and Riches, C. (eds) *Approaches to School Management*. London: Harper Educational Series.

Gleick, J. (1987) *Chaos*. London: Cardinal.

Glover, D. and Law, S. (1995) *The Gloss and the Reality: Changing Professional Practice in Secondary Schools*. Keele University: Keele Professional Development Papers.

Godefroy, C.H. and Clark, J. (1989) *The Complete Time Management System*. London:

Piatkus.

Gordon, L. (1989) Review symposium: governing education. *British Journal of Sociology of Education* **10** (1), 105–9.

Gordon, L. and Pearce, D. (1993) Why compare? A response to Stephen Lawton. *Journal of Education Policy* **8** (2), 175–81.

Goulding, S., Bell, J., Bush, T., Fox, A. and Goodey, J. (1984) *Case Studies in Educational Management*. London: Harper and Row Publishers.

Gramsci, A. (1971) *Selections from the Prison Notebooks*, edited and translated by Hoare, Q. and Nowell Smith, G. New York: International Publishers.

Green, H. (ed.) (1993) *The School Management Handbook 1993*. London: Kogan Page.

Green, H. (ed.) (1994) *The School Management Handbook 1994*. London: Kogan Page.

Green, H. (ed.) (1995) *The School Management Handbook 1995*. London: Kogan Page.

Greenfield, T.B. (1973) Organisations as social inventions: rethinking assumptions about change. *Journal of Applied Behavioural Science* **9** (5) 551–74.

Greenfield, T.B. (1980) The man who comes back through the door in the wall: discovering the truth, discovering self, discovering organisations. *Educational Administration Quarterly* **16** (3), 26–59.

Griffiths, D.E., Weaver Hart, A. and Goode Blair, B. (1991) Still another approach to administration: chaos theory. *Educational Administration Quarterly* **27** (3), 430–51.

Gunter, H. (1996) Appraisal and the school as a learning organisation. *School Organisation* **16** (1), 89–100.

Halpin, D. (1990) Review symposium. *British Journal of Sociology of Education* **11** (4), 473–6.

Halpin, D. and Troyna, B. (eds) (1994) *Researching Education Policy: Ethical and Methodological Issues*. London: Falmer Press.

Hammersley, M. (1992) On feminist methodology. *Sociology* **26** (2), 187–206.

Hammersley, M. and Atkinson, P. (1983) *Ethnography: Principles in Practice*. London: Tavistock Books.

Harding, S. (ed.) (1987) *Feminism and Methodology*. Milton Keynes: Indiana University Press, Indiana/Open University Press.

Hargreaves, A. (1994) *Changing Teachers, Changing Times: Teachers' Work and Culture in the Postmodern Age*. London: Cassell.

Hargreaves, D.H. (1995) Self-managing schools and development planning – chaos or control? *School Organisation* **15** (3), 215–27.

Hargreaves, D.H. and Hopkins, D. (1991) *The Empowered School: the Management and Practice of Development Planning*. London: Cassell.

Harries-Jenkins, G. (1984) Education Management: part 1. *School Organisation and Management Abstracts* **3** (4), 213–33.

Harries-Jenkins, G. (1985) Education Management: part 2. A bibliography. *School Organisation and Management Abstracts* **4** (1), 5–16.

Hatcher, R. (1994) Market relationships and the management of teachers. *British Journal of Sociology of Education* **15** (1), 41–61.

Hatcher, R. and Troyna, B. (1994) The 'policy cycle': a ball by ball account. *Journal of Education Policy* **9** (2), 155–70.

Hayles, N.K. (1990) *Chaos Bound: Orderly Disorder in Contemporary Literature and Science*. New York: Cornell University Press.

Hesse, M. (1980) *Revolutions and Reconstructions in the Philosophy of Science*. Brighton: The Harvester Press.

Higher Education Review (1995) Editorial: The academic profession. *Higher Education Review* **27** (2), 3–7.

Hodgkinson, C. (1978) *Towards a Philosophy of Administration*. Oxford: Basil Blackwell.

Howell, D.A. (1978) *A Bibliography of Educational Administration in the United Kingdom*. Windsor: NFER.

Hoyle, E. (1986) The management of schools: theory and practice. In Hoyle, E. and McMahon, A. *World Yearbook of Education 1986: The Management of Schools*. London: Kogan Page.

Hughes, M.G. (ed.) (1974) *Secondary School Administration: A Management Approach* (second edition). Oxford: Pergamon Press Ltd.

Hughes, M.G. (1978) *Education Administration: Pure or Applied?* Birmingham: University of Birmingham.

Inglis, F. (1985) *The Management of Ignorance*. Oxford: Basil Blackwell.

Jantsch, E. (1980) *The Self-organizing Universe*. Oxford: Pergamon Press.

Jeffers, S. (1991) *Feel the Fear and Do It Anyway*. London: Arrow.

Jenkins, R. (1992) *Pierre Bourdieu*. London: Routledge.

Johnson, P. and Gill, J. (1993) *Management Control and Organizational Behaviour*. London: Paul Chapman.

Johnson, S. (1992) *'Yes' or 'No': The Guide to Better Decisions*. London: Harper Collins.

Jones, J. (1993) *Appraisal and Staff Development in Schools*. London: David Fulton Publishers.

Jones, L. and Moore, R. (1993) Education, competence, and the control of expertise. *British Journal of Sociology of Education* **14** (4), 385–97.

Kemmis, S. (1991) Emancipatory action research and Post Modernisms. *Curriculum Perspectives* **11**, 59–65.

Kent, G. (1989) *The Modern Primary School Headteacher*. London: Kogan Page.

King, R. (1984) School management and the sociology of education. *Education Management and Administration* **12**, 59–62.

Kirkham, G. (1995) Headlamp and the need for an enlightened view of mentoring for new school leaders. *Journal of Educational Administration* **33** (5), 74–83.

Knight, B. (1989) *Managing School Time*. Harlow: Longman.

Kogan, M. (1979) Different frameworks for education policy-making and analysis. *Educational Analysis* **1** (2), 5–14.

Kyriacou, C. (1995) An evaluation of teacher appraisal in schools within one local education authority. *School Organisation* **15** (2), 109–16.

Lane, T. (1995) Patterns of thinking in educational administration. *Journal of Educational Administration* **33** (1), 63–78.

Lather, P. (1986) Research as praxis. *Harvard Educational Review* **56** (3), 257–77.

Lawrence, I. (1994) Master plans. *Times Educational Supplement* November 18, 11.

Lawrence, C.E. and Vachon, M.K. (1995) *How to Handle Staff Misconduct – A Step by Step Guide*. London: Corwen Press.

Lawton, S.B. (1992) Why restructure?: an international survey of the roots of reform. *Journal of Education Policy* **7**(2), 139–54.

Lehrer, R., Serlin, R.C. and Amundson, R. (1990) Knowledge or certainty? A reply to Cziko. *Educational Researcher* August-September, 16–19.

Lewin, R. (1992) *Complexity: Life at the Edge of Chaos*. New York: Macmillan Publishing Company.

Locke, M. (1986) Editorial: Knowing better. *Educational Management and Administration* **14**, 163–5.

Lomax, P. (1995) Action research for professional practice. *British Journal of In-Service Education* **21**(1), 49–57.

Lowe, T.J. and Pollard, I.W. (1989) Negotiation skills. In Riches, C. and Morgan, C. (1989) *Human Resource Management in Education*. Buckingham: Open University Press.

McCarthy, J. and Morrell, J. (1993) *Some Other Rainbow*. London: Bantam Press.

McIllhatton, S., Johnson, N. and Holden, J. (1993) What can educational managers learn from private enterprise? *International Journal of Educational Management* **7**(1), 36–9.

McMahon, A. and Bolam, R. (1990) *A Handbook for Secondary Schools*. London: Paul Chapman Publishing.

McPherson, A. and Raab, C.D. (1989) A prisoner's dilemma: rejoinder to Liz Gordon. *British Journal of Sociology of Education* **10**(4), 475–80.

Maguire, M. and Ball, S.J. (1994) Researching politics and the politics of research: recent qualitative studies in the UK. *Qualitative Studies in Education* **7**(3), 269–85.

Marland, M. (ed.) (1986) *School Management Skills*. London: Heinemann Educational Books.

Marland, M. and Rogers, R. (1991) *Marketing the School*. Oxford: Heinemann Educational.

Maslow, A.H. (1943) A theory of human motivation. *Psychological Review*. **50**(4), 370–96.

Mathias, J. and Jones, J. (1989) *Appraisal of Performance: An Aid to Professional Development*. Windsor: NFER-Nelson.

Mies, M. (1983) Towards a methodology of feminist research. In Bowles, G. and Duelli Klien, R. *Theories of Women's Studies*. London: Routledge and Kegan Paul.

Mills, C.W. (1970) *The Sociological Imagination*. Harmondsworth: Penguin.

Mintzberg, H. (1973) *The Nature of Managerial Work*. New York: Harper and Row.

Mountford, B. (1993) Mentoring and initial teacher education. In Smith, P. and West-Burnham, J. *Mentoring in the Effective School* Harlow: Longman.

Newman, J. and Clarke, J. (1994) Going about our business? The managerialism of public services. In Clarke, J., Cochrane, A. and McLaughlin, E. (1994) *Managing Social Policy*. London: Sage.

Nicholson, J. (1992) *How Do You Manage?* London: BBC/BCA.

Nicholson, R. (1989) *School Management: the Role of the Secondary Headteacher*. London: Kogan Page.

Nilson, T.H. (1995) *Chaos Marketing*. Maidenhead: McGraw-Hill Book Company.

Nonaka, I. (1988) Creating organizational order out of chaos: self-renewal in Japanese firms. *California Management Review* Spring, 57–73.

Oakland, J.S. (1989) *Total Quality Management*. Oxford: Butterworth-Heinemann.

O'Connor, J. (1984) *Accumulation Crisis*. London: Basil Blackwell.

OFSTED (1992) *Handbook for the Inspection of Schools*. London: HMSO.

Ormston, M. and Shaw, M. (1993) *Inspection: A Preparation Guide for Schools*. Harlow: Longman.

Ormston, M. and Shaw, M. (1994) *Inspection: A Preparation Guide for Schools* (second edition). Harlow: Longman.

Osborne, A. (1990) The nature of education management. In Davies, B., Ellison, L., Osborne, A. and West-Burnham, J. (1990) *Education Management for the 1990s*. Harlow: Longman.

Ozga, J. (1987) Studying education policy through the lives of the policymakers: an attempt to close the macro-micro gap. In Walker, S. and Barton, L. *Changing Policies, Changing Teachers: New Directions for Schooling?* Milton Keynes: Open University Press.

Ozga, J. (1990) Policy research and policy theory: a comment on Fitz and Halpin. *Journal of Education Policy* **5** (4), 359–62.

Ozga, J. (1992) Review essay: education management. *British Journal of Sociology of Education* **13**(2), 279–80.

Ozga, J. (1995) Deskilling a profession: professionalism deprofessionalisation and the new managerialism. In Busher, H. and Saran, R. (eds) *Managing Teachers as Professionals in Schools*. London: Kogan Page.

Ozga, J. and Gewirtz, S. (1994) Sex, lies, and audiotape: interviewing the education policy elite. In Halpin, D. and Troyna, B. (eds) *Researching Education Policy: Ethical and Methodological Issues*. London: Falmer Press.

Ozga, J. and Lawn, M. (1988) Schoolwork: interpreting the labour process of teaching. *British Journal of Sociology of Education* **9** (3), 323–36.

Packwood, T. (1977) The school as a hierarchy. *Educational Administration* **5** (2), 1–6. Reprinted in Westoby, A. (ed.) (1988) *Culture and Power in Educational Organizations*. Milton Keynes: Open University Press.

Packwood, T. and Turner, C. (1977) Comments. *Educational Administration* **5** (2), 12–14. Reprinted in Westoby, A. (ed.) (1988) *Culture and Power in Educational Organizations*. Milton Keynes: Open University Press.

Pedlar, M. and Boydell, T. (1985) *Managing Yourself*. London: Fontana.

Pedlar, M., Burgoyne, J. and Boydell, T. (1994) *A Manager's Guide to Self Development* (3rd edn). Maidenhead: McGraw Hill Book Company.

Percival, I. (1991) Chaos: a science for the real world. In Hall, N. (ed.) *The New Scientist Guide to Chaos*. Harmondsworth: Penguin.

Peters, T. (1988) *Thriving on Chaos*. London: Guild Publishing.

Peters, T. and Waterman, R. (1982) *In Search of Excellence*. Glasgow: Harper/Collins.

Playfoot, D., Skelton, M. and Southworth, G. (1989) *The Primary School Management Book*. London: Mary Glasgow Publications Limited.

Pollitt, C. (1992) *Managerialism and the Public Services*. Oxford: Basil Blackwell.

Poster, C. (1976) *School Decision-making: Educational Management in Secondary Schools*. London: Heinemann Educational Books.

Preedy, M. (ed.) (1989) *Teachers' Case Studies in Educational Management*. London: Paul Chapman Publishing Ltd.

Prigogine, I. and Stengers, I. (1984) *Order out of Chaos*. New York: Bantam Books.

Puffitt, R., Stoten, B. and Winkley, D. (1992) *Business Planning for Schools*. Harlow: Longman.

Pugh, D.S. (ed.) (1990) *Organization Theory* (3rd edn). London: Penguin.

Radzicki, M.J. (1990) Institutional dynamics, deterministic chaos, and self-organizing systems. *Journal of Economic Issues* **24** (1), 57–102.

Ramazanoglu, C. (1992) On feminist methodology: male reason versus female empowerment. *Sociology* **26** (2), 207–12.

Richardson, E. (1973) *The Teacher, the School and the Task of Management*. London: Heinemann Educational Books Ltd.

Russell, S. (1994) The 'ah ha' factor. *Education* October 21.

Ryan, B. (1993) 'And your corporate manager will set you free …': devolution in South Australian education. In Smyth, J. (ed.) *A Socially Critical View of the Self-managing School*. London: Falmer Press.

Saul, J.R. (1992) *Voltaire's Bastards*. New York: Free Press.

Savage, W.W. (1989) Communication: process and problems. In Riches, C. and Morgan, C. *Human Resource Management in Education*. Buckingham: Open University Press.

Sawada, D. and Caley, M. (1985) Dissipative structures: new metaphors for becoming in education. *Educational Researcher* **14** (3), 13–19.

Schon, D. (1983) *The Reflective Practitioner: How Professionals Think in Action*. New York: Basic Books.

Semler, R. (1989) Managing without managers. *Harvard Business Review* September-October, 76–84.

Shakeshaft, C. (1987) *Women in Educational Administration*. Newbury Park CA: Sage.

Shulman, L. (1987) Knowledge and teaching: foundations of the new reform. *Harvard Educational Review* **57** (1), 1–22.

Silver, H. (1983) *Education as History: Interpreting Nineteenth and Twentieth Century Education*. London: Methuen.

Silver, H. (1990) *Education, Change and the Policy Process*. Lewes: Falmer.

Smith, P. and West-Burnham, J. (eds) (1993) *Mentoring in the Effective School*. Harlow: Longman.

Smith, R. (1992) *The Heads and Deputies Handbook: Managing Schools in the 1990s*. Lancaster: Framework Press.

Smyth, J. (1992) Teachers' work and the politics of reflection. *American Educational Research Journal* **29** (2), 267–300.

Smyth, J. (ed.) (1993) *A Socially Critical View of the Self-managing School*. London: Falmer Press.

Snyder, K.J., Acker-Hocevar, M. and Wolf, K.M. (1995) Chaos Theory as a Lens for Advancing Quality Schooling. A paper presented to the Annual Conference of the British Educational Management and Administration Society, September 1995.

Sparkes, A.C. and Bloomer, M. (1993) Teaching cultures and school-based management: towards a collaborative reconstruction. In Smyth, J. (ed.) *A Socially Critical View of the Self-managing School*. London: Falmer Press.

Stacey, R.D. (1991) *The Chaos Frontier*. Oxford: Butterworth-Heinemann.

Stacey, R.D. (1992) *Managing Chaos*. London: Kogan Page.

Stacey, R.D. (1993) *Strategic Management and Organisational Dynamics*. London: Pitman.

Stanley, L. and Wise, S. (1983) *Breaking Out: Feminist Consciousness and Feminist Research*. London: Routledge and Kegan Paul.

Stewart, J. and Walsh, K. (1992) Change in the management of public services. *Public Administration* **27**, Winter, 499–518.

Strain, M. (1995) Teaching as a profession: the changing legal and social context. In Busher, H. and Saran, R. (eds) *Managing Teachers as Professionals in Schools*. London: Kogan Page.

Sullivan, T.J. (1994) *System Metamorphosis: An Examination of Chaos Theory Applied to a System of School Organization Undergoing Policy Implementation*. Unpublished Doctoral Thesis, University of New England, Armidale, Australia.

Sungaila, H. (1990a) The new science of chaos: making a new science of leadership? *Journal of Educational Administration* **28**(2), 4–23.

Sungaila, H. (1990b) Organizations alive: have we at last found the key to a science of educational administration? *Studies in Educational Administration* No 52, May, Commonwealth Council for Educational Administration.

Taylor, F.W. (1911) *Principles of Scientific Management*. New York: Harper.

Thody, A. (1993) *Developing Your Career in Education Management*. Harlow: Longman.

Toffler, A. (1984) Science and change. Foreword to Prigogine, I. and Stengers, I. (1984) *Order out of Chaos*. New York: Bantam Books.

Trethowan, D. (1985) *Teamwork*. London: Industrial Society Press.

Trotter, A. (1993) *Better Self-management: A Handbook for Education Staff*. Harlow: Longman.

Troyna, B. (1994a) Critical social research and education policy. *British Journal of Educational Studies* **42** (1), 70–84.

Troyna, B. (1994b) Reforms, research and being reflexive about being reflective. In Halpin, D. and Troyna, B. (eds) *Researching Education Policy: Ethical and Methodological Issues*. London: Falmer Press.

Troyna, B. and Williams, J. (1986) *Racism, Education and the State*. Beckenham: Croom Helm.

Turner, C. (1977) Organising educational institutions as anarchies. *Educational Administration* **5**(2), 6–12. Reprinted in Westoby, A. (ed.) (1988) *Culture and Power in*

Educational Organizations. Milton Keynes: Open University Press.

Ury, W. (1991) *Getting Past No*. London: Business Books.

Walford, G. (1993) Self-managing schools, choice and equity. In Smyth, J. (ed.) *A Socially Critical View of the Self-managing School*. London: Falmer Press.

Walford, G. (1994) Political commitment in the study of the City Technology College, Kingshurst. In Halpin, D. and Troyna, B. (eds) *Researching Education Policy: Ethical and Methodological Issues*. London: Falmer Press.

Wallace, M. and Hall, V. (1994) *Inside the SMT: Teamwork in Secondary School Management*. London: Paul Chapman Publishing.

Walters, B. (1994) *Management for Special Needs*. London: Cassell.

Watson, L.E. (1982) The management of education in its social setting. In Gray, H.L. (ed.) *The Management of Educational Institutions: Theory, Research, Consultancy*. Lewes: Falmer Press.

Weick, K.E. (1976) Educational organizations as loosely coupled education. *Administrative Science Quarterly* **21**, 1–19.

Weick, K.E. (1988) Educational organizations as loosely coupled systems. In Westoby, A. (ed.) (1988) *Culture and Power in Educational Organizations*. Milton Keynes: Open University Press.

West, M. and Bollington, R. (1990) *Teacher Appraisal – A Practical Guide for Schools*. London: David Fulton Publishers.

West-Burnham, J. (1992) *Managing Quality in Schools*. Harlow: Longman.

Wheatley, M.J. (1994) *Leadership and the New Science*. San Francisco: Berrett-Koehler Publications Inc.

Whitaker, P. (1993) *Managing Change in Schools*. Buckingham: Open University Press.

White, C. and Crump, S. (1993) Education and the three 'P's: policy, politics and practice. A review of the work of S.J. Ball. *British Journal of Sociology of Education* **14** (4), 415–29.

White, P. (1987) Self-respect, self-esteem and the management of educational institutions: a question of values. *Educational Management and Administration* **15**, 85–91.

Winter, R. (1991) Post-modern sociology as a democratic educational practice? Some suggestions. *British Journal of Sociology of Education* **12**(4), 467–81.

Name index

Subject index